Praise for *I'll Know It When I See It*

"A tour de force. A powerful, earthy, affectionate story whose disparate sections are knit together by Carey's skillful characterizations, authentic dialogue, and witty observations."

–Kirkus Reviews

"A wryly entertaining meditation on the many ways in which you can go home again. At its heart, this is a Cinderella story in which a maid remains a maid but is transformed nonetheless."

–New York Times Book Review

"[Carey] is such a skillful writer that the very light changes as she moves from New York to Ireland. Language changes, too, from the crisp rhythms of New York to the melodic tones of County Cork. What is ultimately enchanting about the book is that it has its own music behind a story that makes you want to say, 'More, more.'"

–Frank McCourt, author of Angela's Ashes and 'Tis

"In her outstanding literary debut, Alice Carey searches for a place to call home. *I'll Know It When I See It* is an engaging memoir that moves seamlessly from New York City to rural Ireland, from Carey's 1950s childhood to the 1990s of her middle age. All the while, Carey skillfully explores issues of family, cultural identity, and belonging."

—Denver Post

"As a first-generation émigré returning to her mother's land, Alice Carey has written an enchanting tale of dreams lost and found."

—Jeremy Irons, actor

"A sweet and funny book about searching out the home of your dreams at age 50. Readers will rejoice as they find their true home."

—Times-Picayune

I'LL KNOW IT
WHEN I SEE IT

I'LL KNOW IT
WHEN I SEE IT

A Daughter's Search
for Home in Ireland

Alice Carey

SEAL PRESS

I'll Know It When I See It
A Daughter's Search for Home in Ireland

The author and publisher gratefully acknowledge permission to reprint the following material: "The Lake Isle of Innisfree" by William Butler Yeats. Reprinted with the permission of Scribner, a division of Simon & Schuster, Inc., and A.P. Watt, Ltd., on behalf of Michael B. Yeats. From *The Collected Works of W.B. Yeats*, Volume 1: *The Poems, Revised*, edited by Richard J. Finneran (New York: Scribner, 1997), published in the U.K, by A.P. Watt, Ltd. "The Isle of Innisfree" by Richard Farrelly © 1950, renewed 1978 by Universal Music Corp./ASCAP. Used by Permission. International Copyright Secured. All Rights Reserved.

All photographs are from the author's private collection.
Photos and illustrations are used by permission and are the property of the original copyright owners.

Published by Seal Press
An Imprint of Avalon Publishing Group, Incorporated
1400 65th Street, Suite 250
AVALON
publishing group incorporated
Emeryville, CA 94608

Cataloging-in-publication data has been applied for.

ISBN 1-58005-132-4

9 8 7 6 5 4 3 2 1

Cover design by Stewart Williams
Interior design by Justin Marler
Printed in the United States of America by Malloy
Distributed by Publishers Group West

To the fairies who made it possible and
the BVM who saw it through.

i will arise and go now

THERE IS NOTHING SO SCARY yet enticing to a young girl as a fairy tale where another girl is kept captive in a tower until she is rescued. And once upon a time, there was nothing more scary and enticing to me than to know my picture was held captive in a room with the spirits of the dead.

Mammie and I have come back to Ireland for a visit. It's taken us a week to get here on the RMS *Mauretania*.

"O Alice M'rie," she says over and over, "we're going Home."

Everybody says it. No one can say boo in Ireland without sticking "Home" in somewhere. They imbue it with meaning. *Home* . . . and they lower the voice as if they are saying *God*.

O Alice, ye're finally *Home*.

It's good to be *Home*.

Everyone at *Home* is looking forward to ye.

. . . and ye've brought Alice M'rie *Home* with ye.

It is the early sixties. Aer Lingus is flying across the Atlantic in green planes. The Beatles are getting popular. JFK is President. And Mammie has finally saved up enough

2

money in a Christmas Club to take me, her twelve-year-old daughter, Home. She is going to show me off to what's left of her family in County Kerry.

"O Alice M'rie," she's been saying for years, "we must save some more so we can go *Home* next year."

Home . . . It should mean something good to me, but it doesn't. It means something good to Mammie.

Home: You would think she'd be sick of the word. In New York Mammie couldn't wait to run out the door of the place we called home, away from Carey, as we called my father. *Home*. The way Mammie goes on, you'd think we were going to visit one of those old castles pictured on postcards.

The car stops at a brand-new two-story bungalow on the side of the road. The view is pretty; the house is not. *Home*. Is this what we saved and saved to see? Smack up against the house is what Mammie must be thinking about when she says *Home*. Next to the new house is the old thatched cottage where Alice Slattery, my mother, was born.

It's taken us all day to get here, and now that we're here, everyone stands around the kitchen with their coats on. There's Mammie's two brothers—Father Bob, the priest, and David, the farmer. There's Dave's wife, Mary Falvey—never referred to as just Mary, or Mrs. Slattery, but always Mary Falvey—and their two sons, D.D. and Robert, my cousins. Mary Falvey's just paid me a compliment that's music to Mammie's ears.

3

"O Alice M'rie," she said, "ye don't sound like a Yank. Ye sound just like yer mother."

A turf fire fails to combat the damp. The kettle is on the hob, and small glasses of whiskey are being passed around. Mammie is the center of attention.

"O Alice, ye've come *Home*," they say, grabbing her hands as if she were a bishop.

Mammie's home is plain. It's neither painted nor heated. It has no books. No TV. No magazines. A few scraggly geraniums sit in a window. On a kitchen shelf a radio and a portrait of the Sacred Heart vie for attention. The kitchen serves as living room and scullery. The floor is cement. They do all their living here. I've been warned we'll have to use chamber pots, since there's no bathroom. Brack the sheepdog wanders around, and a little pregnant cat looks like she'll not live to nurse her kittens.

Mammie, Father Bob, and Dave are laughing away.

. . . and who else is coming *Home* this summer?

She misses *Home*, that one.

Nothing's changed at *Home*.

It's an early summer evening and I'm rambling about. This will be my home for the next month and I'm stuck. Stuck! No walking out to the corner newsstand to check up on the latest magazines in this place. And get rid of those thoughts of castles and fairies. This is modern Ireland. Make the best of it. Offer it up. Mammie is happy and I will be, too.

4

I traipse from one bedroom to another. They're all alike. Bed and a light, bed and a light. At least Mammie and I have the room with the view and a table. Downstairs the doors are all ajar, except for the room next to the front door. Not one for leaving stones unturned, I open it.

Crack it gently. Slip in. Can't let them hear me in the kitchen. Light from a single window casts a feeble glow on a formal room whose decor doesn't match the rest of the house. Taking up most of the space is a large dining table covered by a linen cloth. Atop that is an empty crystal fruit bowl. Around the perimeter are a few pieces of upholstered furniture smack up against the wall, a dresser crammed with what looks to be the good china, and a sideboard covered with pictures.

The pictures, old black-and-whites called snaps, catch my eye. Scattered throughout them are holy cards: one side with a picture of Mother Mary, the other a passport-sized photo of a person.

I go from woman to man to child to priest to nun, as though the people in the pictures are calling out to me. Then it hits me. All these people are dead. They must be dead, for they're all wearing clothes from other eras. Do I know any of them? I must know some of them. Some of them look like me. That woman with a bun on her head and a very big nose must be Mammie's mother. The man in a cap leaning against a rick of hay, her father. There's her sister, Mollie, the nun, whose name Mammie always prefaces with "O poor" because Mollie died of leukemia. Then I saw them. Pushed to the rear were pictures of Mammie and me.

Studio portraits taken the day of my First Communion and Confirmation. And snaps. There's Mammie and me standing in the street before we went into Manhattan to see *My Fair Lady*. (I used to think to myself that I could die happy, now that I had finally seen *My Fair Lady*.) There's Mammie and me sitting on the front stoop of our flat in Queens. There's Mammie and me all dolled up on our way to Mass. There are no pictures of Carey.

I know I am trespassing but I don't care. I'm half blind from the dark and terrified the Slatterys will come in and find me. Yet the power of these pictures holds me in that room. The only piece of decorative art is a large, framed lithograph called *The Three Blind Children at the Holy Well*, presiding over the sideboard.

Depicted are three little girls in rags and tatters, dipping their hands into an old stone well, and smiling up to heaven with beatific, closed-eyed smiles. It's fabulous. It's spooky. I can't take my eyes off it. It fits in with all the gory fairy tales I love, the ones where girls are blinded or maimed until they are redeemed, like *The Little Mermaid*. But what is especially wonderful about *The Three Blind Children at the Holy Well* is that Mammie's and my pictures are propped up there underneath it.

"Alice M'rie, where are ye? Come in for the tea."

Trembling with excitement, I head back to the kitchen. They haven't even missed me.

I tell not a soul. It's my secret as well as my ignorance. I don't know why we've been lumped in there with the dead, but I love that we are. I can't wait for my daily peek. When they go out for the cows, I go in for a look. There are the girls and there am I, all joined together in a lovely, creepy alliance.

After a week of subterfuge, I know I have to try to wheedle the *why* out of Mammie. We'd be lying in bed at night and she'd ask, she'd always ask, "Well then, Alice M'rie, what do ye think of *Home*?"

"Oh, it's great it is. It's so different. So nice and quiet."

When I finally broach it, I doubt she suspects a thing. "Mammie, ye know that room, that room that's closed down there by the door? Do they not use it at all?"

I've picked the right time for my question, for Mammie is so involved with the Duchess of Windsor's book, *The Heart Has Its Reasons*, she barely looks up.

"O Alice M'rie, ye best not be going in there at all. There'll be time enough for that our last night, when we'll have dinner in there."

"But why is it closed up?"

"It's for wakes. They call it the West Room. Long ago they used to say that when people died, their souls headed west so they could live with the fairies and always stay young. That's what they said. And I don't know if it's true at all. It's a *pisherogue*. But they do put pictures of people who died in there, so they can look down from heaven and pray for us."

That's all Mammie says. She doesn't say why we are there. Nor do I ask.

And go to innisfree

THAT WAS LONG AGO.

Years later, long after Mammie died and Father Bob and Dave Slattery died, years later, when the Slattery bungalow softened into the landscape, and the old house—the place Mammie called *Home*—housed farm machinery and chickens, years later, when I grew up, my husband and I bought an old house in Ireland with a West Room.

It is a blow-winds-and-crack-your-cheeks November night in County Cork. The wind is howling off Bantry Bay and bouncing off the chimney pots of Bantry House, where my husband, Geoffrey Knox, and I are the only guests. We've spent the day looking at houses and are now sitting in front of a blazing turf fire. I'm nursing a double Irish whiskey, hoping it'll warm me up. Geoffrey has a pint. He thinks I've disgraced myself by ordering Paddy (the proletarian *craythur*).

"Bushmills," he says. "Bushmills is the good stuff."

This from a man who doesn't know one whiskey from another. Bushmills, I tell him, is made in Northern Ireland. I'll order it when there's peace in Ireland.

Spread out on a Chinese lacquered table are Polaroid pictures of an old bang of a house we're thinking

10

of buying. Just like that! Snap of the fingers. Impulsive? Yes. For it's on a whim and a prayer we've come over to Ireland, on a Thanksgiving weekend, in hopes of finding our hearts' desire, a house in Ireland.

Why I want a house here is a mystery to me, for I've no romance at all about the place. In fact, when I grab myself by the scruff of the neck and say, Wait a minute, Alice M'rie, what'erye doing *back* here? answers fail me. It's not blood relations that bring me back. Blame it then on a snowy winter that found Geoffrey and me at home in New York in front of our fireplace, idling nights away, thinking thoughts of the future.

With the millennium hovering, Geoffrey wanted to know where I'd like to be at the end of the century. I suppose I could have said something romantic, like "Why, darling, any old place with you," and launched into a chorus of "When I'm 64," but I didn't. Instead, I confessed that by the millennium I wanted to be living in some place other than New York City.

As the words came out of my mouth, little snakes of guilt crept up from the floorboards at the thought of defection. Real New Yorkers never admit that they just *might* like living somewhere else. Anyway, my confession made, Geoffrey grinned and said, "Me too." In a heart-beat, we knew our destiny.

That winter it seemed that all we talked about were places. Every place we visited as students. Every place we saw in the movies. Every place that had a song written about it. To fuel these geographical fantasies, Geoffrey and I played records. We'd name a place and sing the song. Hate California, it's cold and it's damp. Lady of Spain, I adore you. We're off on the road to Morocco. (We couldn't find a song for Switzerland but it wasn't on the list anyway.) Then we drew up our lists of countries to see where we matched.

On the night in question we were listening to Frank Sinatra singing "The fire will dwindle into glowing ashes, for flame and love will never die." It's the "glowing ashes" that secures the image of us in my head. Separately, mind, like little children writing wish lists, our hands shielding our dreams from each other's prying eyes, we each wrote down Ireland. It was the only country we both chose. That was it. In a lightning bolt of faith we knew we'd hit upon the land of heart's desire.

Ireland. As odd as it was appropriate, for Ireland was the first place Geoffrey and I had visited together. In 1976, when we were new lovers, we hitched around, ran out of money, had a terrible time, and vowed never to return. In a change of heart we returned in 1990 to find Ireland finally catching up with the twentieth century, as the rest of the world was galloping toward the twenty-first. I began to see Ireland as *Ireland* rather than just the country Mammie and Carey came from.

The following year we went to Dublin for New Year's Eve, and returned the next for another shot of welcoming in the year dancing to "Mustang Sally." Ireland had changed. The Celtic Tiger was in residence in every county from Kerry to Donegal. His kittens drove around in new cars, shopped at Benetton, ate Häagen-Dazs ice cream, went to the mall, rouged their lips with Lancôme, swam at leisure centers, and shopped at Los Angeles–sized supermarkets. Ireland had grown up and changed, as had I.

So there we were at Bantry House looking at a shiver-me-timbers set of Polaroids of an old farmhouse we're falling in love with outside a nearby village. There I am, pointing with glee to an old house you can barely see in the dark. There's Geoffrey, trying to free a ram from a blackberry thicket. There's a sickly calf, with its head sticking out of a hole in a derelict stable. There's a crumbling fireplace big enough to roast a pig. Here's a nice one, the sun coming out for an Irish minute, on the house on a ridge lined with large old trees. The house looks like Manderley.

We've been on the go since we left New York on Thanksgiving Eve, and as Mammie used to say, I've not had the time to bless myself. Before going to sleep I play with the snapshots one more time, shuffling them like a deck of playing cards, hoping they'll form a clearer picture. Geoffrey looks at Ireland differently from the way I do. I think he has to. He's American and completely besotted with the place. I don't know what to think. Now that I'm here, I feel a little sad. And I'm wide awake. Geoffrey is sound asleep.

The tolling of the clock on the battlements of Bantry House takes me to another island, this one off the coast of Long Island. To a sandbar called Fire Island and a village there called Cherry Grove. We have spent practically every weekend on Fire Island for the last twenty years. This is the first Thanksgiving we've not roasted a turkey there.

If it's one in the morning in Ireland, it's eight in the evening in Cherry Grove. The *Herald Tribune* says the weather's nice and warm in New York. If we were there, we'd have the screen door open onto the deck, the sound of the ocean soothing our souls. So why are you here, if your heart is still there? No matter what countries you wrote on that list, admit it, you love the Island. But I changed. Fire Island changed. And Geoffrey changed. AIDS changed everything. Will you be on the Island for Thanksgiving? they were asking us on the Cherry Grove ferry last weekend. No, we're going to Ireland. Ireland? *Ireland*? Don't they shoot people over there? Magic Flute, our little Arts and Crafts house in the Grove, is lonely, catless, flowerless, and wineless this weekend. To be able to afford to buy a house in Ireland, we'll probably have to sell Magic Flute.

Two o'clock and I must get up. It's pitch black outside. If we were on the Island, Geoffrey and I might be dancing out on the deck under the bare-limbed cherry tree, listening to old records. This is an island. That is an island. Why are we thinking of moving from one island to another?

14

"Geoffrey . . . you awake? I can't sleep. I keep thinking of the house. . . ."

"Which house?"

"*Our* house . . . how we might be dancing on the deck."

The clock strikes three. Geoffrey has gotten up. I can't see him, nor he me. When it's dark in Ireland, it's dark.

"I miss that part of us."

"What part of us? I'm here."

"I mean the us out there at the beach. Once we leave, it'll all be gone. I'll miss us standing on the top deck, listening to the train whistles on Long Island. What will we listen to here, in the still of the night?"

And I laugh, for even in the midst of despair, as always, my reference is song. Geoffrey puts his arms around me and we start singing and dancing in place. We both know "In the still of the night, when the world is in slumber."

"We'll listen to the silence and hear new things."

"Promise."

With that, a boat whistles on Bantry Bay.

"See?"

By five the storm breaks, and by eight a pink winter dawn lights the battlements and the bay. It's a Friday, Market Day in Bantry. *Our town*, as we're starting to call it. Now if I were a Bantry citizen out to do weekend shopping, I'd take a quick gander at Geoffrey

15

and me, deem us "blow-ins" (West Cork lingo for strangers), and declare There goes the neighborhood.

We stand out in our black, black, black New York City outfits, for no matter what bill of goods the J. Peterman catalog foists on American women, with those black cloaks made in Galway, Irish women do not wear black. And Irish men wear black only for funerals. Anyway, the two of us are laughing away to beat the band, so giddy with the idea of buying an old house we barely saw in the dark, you'd think we were getting it for free.

Pedophilia is hissing on the airwaves. Seems Taoiseach Albert Reynolds's government is being brought down by old allegations involving an uncensored pedophile priest and his altar boys. Gay Byrne, the Larry King of Irish radio, has everyone's ear. Pee-dough-fee-lee-ia, pee-dough-fee-lee-ia is repeated in a litany by citizens thrilled to be wallowing in another titillating scandal. From Derry to Kerry the Irish are telling Gay Byrne what a terrible t'ing it is. "A man o' God . . . Y'ed t'ink he'd know better." Sure he would. Father Bob pops into my head and I see my twelve-year-old self. O, it's a terrible t'ing. Then I erase the picture with my imaginary chalkboard eraser.

Bantry is hopping. From the stalls and vans that surround Wolfe Tone Square, people are selling everything from live to fresh-killed chickens, to olives, to boots, to cabbages, to hardware, to antiques, to olive oil, to lavender, to primroses, even to ponies. Geoffrey and I stroll about arm in arm, deeming every chicken wonderful, every olive better than any we ever ate in France.

Our actions, as well as our garb, single us out. We're fast, urban walkers. The Irish amble. The click of our heels matches the click of our brains. Is this good? Is this bad? Is Bantry a dreary town with nothing but the hiss of pedophilia to animate it? Or is Bantry a town we can see ourselves living in, driving in to shop on Market Day?

The weather is shaping up. A fresh early winter wind has cleared away the clouds that covered the surrounding hills to reveal lavishly green pastures ringed with stone walls and dotted with sheep. Geoffrey and I stride forward. Up one street, down another. Barrack to Marino to Main to High to Bridge to Church to Glen garriff. In the butcher shops, men wearing straw hats and blue striped aprons lay out pounds of lamb cutlets. At a bakery, women with toddlers gossip over their elevenses coffee. The large supermarket and the smaller one sell De Cecco pasta and wine. Two elegant pharmacies dispense Yardley and Revlon. Several paper shops sell (oh, t'ank God) the *Herald Tribune* and the English papers. And (oh, t'ank God) there's the Bantry Bookstore—a Dickensian one at that, with new and used books.

Gay Byrne is everywhere. From opened shop doors comes the drone. "Oh, 'tis . . . Oh, 'tis . . . Oh, 'tis a sad t'ing . . . pee-dough-fee-lee-ia is a disgrace on the country." Yet despite that we like Bantry.

17

After an elevenses ourselves, we drive back into the countryside for another look at the farmhouse. We note that once past the cemetery at the end of town, it takes but twenty minutes. We need another look. A better look. A determining look. An is-it-worth-it-in-the-long-run-and-if-it-is-we'll-bargain-you-down look, aimed directly at the Key Properties agent handling the house. He was a little bantam rooster who had smugly inquired whether we were interested in a ruin or a bungalow.

I wanted to scream, You fool, you varlet! How can I tell you what I want, when I know you're laughing at another pair of rich Americans, for that's what you think of us? How can I tell you I want a house whose stones were already frosted with moss when Queen Mebh had yet to be buried in Sligo? How can I tell you I want a house whose occupants once spoke Irish? A house built long before Joyce wrote one word. A house where the fairies visit. A house with ghosts. A house whose origins are not of the twentieth century.

"We want an old house."

"Oh den, ye want a ruin."

A fleet of cows munching primroses block the grouted track that serves as a road to this "ruin." And since you can't budge cows, we sit in the car listening to more discussion of pedophilia. (This time the priest himself is on, God help us.) We gaze at the house sitting up there on a ridge. It has been abandoned for years. From our book of place names, we figure out that in Irish, the townland (as Mammie's home in Carrigeen is a townland) means "ridge of the little fox." What was the house's story? Who built it? Why? And why has no one lived in it since (we later find out) 1935? Then, since cows win (they always do), we leave the car, walk up the hill, and climb into the house through a hole that was once a window. Just as we did the evening before.

As we do in bookstores, antique malls, and junkyards, Geoffrey and I separate. He explores here; I there. Yet even through three-feet-thick walls, I can hear his brain clicking away, as I'm sure he hears mine.

Geoffrey thinks: Boy, this is beautiful. No electricity. No plumbing. There's so much to fix, it will take years and years! This will be the project for the rest of our lives! Look at those stone steps going up to a hayloft! Look at all this land/space/birds/sky/valleys/hills/rocks/mountains/water. And no one's around to bother me. This is Ireland. This is great. This is where I want to live the rest of my life.

But I think: An AGA would be nice here. A Shabby Chic couch there. William Morris wallpaper. Climbing roses . . . and a cat, maybe. What am I doing here? I love Fire Island. I don't know what I'll do without it. Will my friends forget me? Will I forget my friends? I don't know how we'll afford this place without selling Magic Flute. I don't know what I'll do without my other island.

The brambly ram is back, looking like King Lear on the heath. The cows too. The sun shines through the broken windows. A few barn swallows, irritated by our presence, dive-bomb our heads. The leaves are changing to red and gold. Autumn, "season of mists and mellow fruitfulness," has o'ertaken the greensward that is Ireland.

The house was stripped of its furniture, yet shadows remain on the walls. The outlines of a large dresser in the kitchen, a wardrobe in an upstairs bedroom, carpet on the stairs. Around the kitchen window, mildewed plaster drips green ooze. Yet the timbered ceiling of the West Room is sound. I go around snipping pieces from shards of wallpaper that once dressed the rooms. Blue and pink roses in the boudoir. Red chinoiserie in a tiny room called the "box room," no bigger than a box, where a child might have slept. The West Room is perfect, smaller than the one in Carrigeen, with a single window that once was shuttered. The fireplace mantel is intact. And if we cleaned out all the birds' nests in all the fireplaces, we might get good fires going in the . . . one, two, three, four fireplaces!

The day is flying. New York is beckoning. Do we make Bantam Rooster an offer? The house, which we've begun calling the Big House, including its outbuildings and three acres, is only £35,000 (around U.S. $50,000). "Only?" I say. It seems affordable. But is it practical? It has no plumbing. No electricity. There isn't a telephone pole in sight. Geoffrey's high-school drama teacher predicted we'd have an "international lifestyle" one day. Yet this is not so much "lifestyle" as it is a dream. A dream with consequence.

With night falling, we walk the land, blinking into the violet-green twilight. At best the property has a faded grandeur. At worst it looks like an Irish dog patch. Beneath the ridge in front of the Big House lies an overgrown cobbled laneway, bordered by hedgerows, linking it to the outbuildings. They are the real ruins. The crumbled buildings relate to one another like a small village, which they once were. In the eighteenth century, several families lived in this *clachán*—a townland of one-room stone dwellings clustered around a central courtyard. And it was the laneway that joined this *clachán* to another.

"Geoffrey," I say suddenly, "this looks like a Famine Village."

The scene reminds me of the cover of *The Great Hunger*, by Cecil Woodham-Smith, one of the few books we had in Astoria when I was a girl. (It remained by the telephone, unopened and avoided.) Father Bob bought it for me in a paper shop in Killarney. I remember him saying, in that way he had of gesturing with his nicotine-stained hand, that I *especially* should know about *It*. Back then no one dared use the word *Famine*. They all said *It*. And Mammie didn't even use *It*. She never, ever let on a thing. Neither she nor Carey ever mentioned the Famine. Yet they must have felt it in their bones. Their grandparents lived through it.

The Famine lasted a brief five years (1845 to 1850), yet even today its effects are felt in Ireland. The Irish Catholics who lived in these *clacháns* would have been the tenant farmers for the English Protestants living in the Big House. Their sole nourishment and crop—the only crop they were allowed to grow by law—was the potato. One summer a potato blight spread across Ireland. From the Atlantic coast to the Bog of Allen, up to the mountains of Mourne and down to the port of Cork, all Ireland was perfumed by the smell of decaying potatoes. Without the potato, which people ate at every meal, the Irish tenant farmers starved. Without the potato, which was used as currency, the Catholics fell in arrears with the rent due to the Protestants, who owned the land. And so their small cottages were razed.

With no civil rights, the Irish had little recourse but to emigrate. More than a million people died during the Famine. Those who survived and arrived on the "coffin ships" at the ports of New York, Boston, Charleston, and elsewhere were referred to as "the wild geese."

The resemblance of *The Great Hunger*'s cover to the spot where Geoffrey and I are standing is scary. Depicted in the Romantic style of nineteenth-century Irish paintings, the image on the book was of a barefoot young woman with long black hair, wearing a green shawl. She was standing alone in the rubble of a one-room stone house by the side of the road. Galloping off to a nearby cottage was a troop of English soldiers—the soldiers who had leveled, or "tumbled," her home. The woman stood clenching her fist to heaven.

This cluster of cottages is the Famine.

This is my bloodline.

It finally hits home.

We are standing in the remains of cottages that had been tumbled during the Famine. From where we are, we can clearly see the Big House, the code word for Protestant house, up on the ridge that swoops down to this courtyard.

We're bolted to the spot, transfixed by the proximity of poor to rich in the rubble of the smallest cottage. A gable wall is still standing, as is the bottom outline of a door. From what was once a window opening, we can see a part of the wall of an adjoining cottage. Across the courtyard stands a bigger, one-room-wide "long house" that was extended laterally, a room at a time, over the years. The remaining roof tiles overlap like purple fish scales. There are gaping holes for the windows and doors. The house is girdled by bog grass and is sinking into the mud.

All is terrible. All is pretty. And it's terrible that it's pretty, with the stones covered in thick, green velvet moss, threaded through with ivy, adding a Victorian grace as they balance atop one another as delicately as seashells.

A small, oratory-shaped structure catches my eye. The limb of an elderberry tree is growing across the space where the roof was. The door opening is so low to the ground, I have to stoop way down to enter; I then stand on the remains of a cobbled stone floor. The structure is barely four feet wide and has no windows, yet the gable end is high enough to comfortably accommodate someone six feet tall.

"Geoffrey," I say, "this looks like a hermitage. Maybe a monk prayed here."

Across the yard stands an old well enclosed by stone walls. Not a Snow White wishing well, but an enclosed spring providing water for this *clachán* that predated the Big House.

Sadness seems to hang heavy in the air. We are not in neutral territory. Geoffrey and I are trespassing on a part of Ireland's bloody past. For regardless of our good intentions to buy this property and honor its past, we realize we are in a place of violence. Light from the west throws a pink glow on the stones. This is the same light, same stone walls, same thicket of trees that were here when the cottages were razed.

I imagine a Protestant family up at the Big House, gathering around the hearth in the parlor on a cool November night like this, drinking tea and playing the piano. From the first floor they can see this *clachán*. They are most likely using the "long house" for their cows, horses, and donkey cart. Yet if there were any Catholics living here at all, they hadn't a pot to piss in.

I start to think of Mammie. I conjure her up as a rather chic young woman with a twenties bob, running from the old house in Carrigeen to New York to seek her future. Her dream had been to own a house in America. Yet she and Carey had never been able to afford one. Maybe he didn't even want one; I don't know. We never talked about things like owning a house, for fear we'd be "above our station." And here I am looking at these old houses, whilst already owning a perfectly good one in America. And my mammie never owned anything. I hope she'd be happy for me. Yet I don't know. The Irish are a begrudging lot. She might be jealous.

Night has fallen. We have a plane to catch in the morning. And possibly an offer to tender to Bantam Rooster. As Geoffrey and I drive to Bantry House, my mind spins back to New York, to when Mammie was a maid cleaning other people's houses. I have to tell the story again. The story of how Mammie became Big Alice, the maid, and I became Little Alice, the little maid. Geoffrey knows the story by heart. He's heard it far too often over the years. Yet I have to tell it again. The guilt, my rising above my station, makes me tell him and myself the story one more time.

CAREY JUST HAD A PHONE INSTALLED in our apartment in Astoria, Queens, and when it rings we are stunned. An emergency is what it's for. That's what Carey says. Mammie's even more stunned to hear the voice of an old crony of hers.

"Alice," says Mary O'Neil, "are ye looking for work? If ye are, there's this thee-atical woman in Manhattan looking for someone to serve at poker parties."

Without hesitating, Mammie says yes. Carey begins screaming and banging doors. Mitzi, my cat, and I flee to my room and lean out the window into the arms of my beautiful cherry tree.

"But D., it'll help."

She's calling him D. Not Denis. Sometimes she calls him Carey. Sometimes he's called "the Great D.D." That's what he calls himself. I never call him anything. I say nothing at all to him, unless we're fighting.

"Oh, it's thee-aticals now, is it? This isn't good enough f'r ye. Huh . . . Huh . . ."

Carey starts running around the apartment. Off go the lights. On go the faucets. Darkness and water. Walpurgisnacht.

"But D., Alice M'rie needs—"

"Alice M'rie needs nothing. She's as bad as ye. Selfish is what she is. Selfish the both of ye."

Mitzi and I march back into the living room. "Don't ye talk that way to my mammie."

"Back talk. Back talk. That's all I get here. That's what ye've taught 'er." I run into the kitchen to turn on the ceiling light. Carey runs after me, grabs my wrist, and bangs it against the sink.

"That'll teach ye to turn on the lights."

Lily McCann, the Belfast woman who lives next

door, starts banging on the wall. Mitzi crouches under the sink and lashes out at Carey's ankles. Carey kicks Mitzi. Mammie yells at me to go to my room. I don't cry. Worse has happened to me. Worse, I tell you. I grab Mitzi, go into my room, and lean out the window to my tree in the landlord's yard.

"Denis, this is why I'm going."

Carey runs down the stairs and out. *Bang!* goes the door. *Bang!* goes the kettle. That's what Mammie does. That's what the Irish do. Tea solves everything. I still believe this. I come out of my room and run my wrist under the cold water.

"Mammie, can't I go with you?"

"Not yet," says Mammie.

That night my mammie lands herself a job as Miss Jean Dalrymple's maid. Life is never the same again. Mammie says Jean Dalrymple is famous. She came from New Jersey, and though she didn't go to college, she became one of the few female producers (in that era) of Broadway plays. Jean-Paul Sartre's *Red Gloves* starring Charles Boyer was the most famous. She is now the Director of the New York City Center Light Opera Company, which is housed in an old mosque on West Fifty-fifth Street. Neither Mammie nor I know what a mosque is.

Mammie starts off by helping out at poker parties. Then a few afternoons a week. Then all day. Carey pretty much stops talking to the two of us, which is a relief. He spends more and more evenings out. By the time he comes home, we're already in bed.

I start going into the city after school to meet Mammie. I've gotten my first glimpse of glamour, and I'm mad for it. Over there across the East River. Beyond the rocks and rats. On the other side of Welfare Island. Below Gracie Mansion. Just a few minutes' walk from Lexington Avenue is a house where everything is lovely. There they call Mammie Big Alice, though she's not very big at all. They call me Little Alice.

"This house is called a town house," says Mammie, thrilled to be intoning "towwwnn house."

We're sitting in Miss D.'s gray, yellow, and blue kitchen. I've just come in from school to help Mammie out. That's what I tell old Mrs. Ritter, who corners me running to the el.

"I'm going into the city to help my mammie out."

"Now you be careful," says Mrs. Ritter, not knowing I'm invincible. Invincible, carrying my copy of the *Reader's Digest*, from whence springs all my knowledge.

My job today is polishing the silver. There's an ice bucket proclaiming *To JD with Love and Admiration the Cast of South Pacific*. Then Mammie puts on the kettle and I eat my snack, a small can of Bumble Bee tuna in oil, not water, for the "pro-teen," as Mammie says. This is special. Tuna fish is special. Mammie says so. No one eats tuna fish in Ireland.

"This house was bought for Miss D. by José Iturbi, the pee-nist. The country house in Connecticut"—O country house, what a beautiful pairing of words—"was bought for Miss D. by Henry Luce, Clare Boothe Luce's husband—"

"Go on! Husband? Henry is married? That's a sin."

"Miss D.'s not a Catholic. It's no sin for her."

(My first lesson in love.)

The phone rings. It's . . . Zsa Zsa Gabor, Fernando Lamas, Arlene Dahl. Unpronounceable names. Un-Irish names. No one in Astoria has names as exotic as these. These people aren't named after saints, and they're none the worse for it.

The more names Mammie adds to her vocabulary, the happier she is. These are the names of important people. Saying them properly is Mammie's substitute for the Litanies.

Virgin most venerable
Virgin most prudent
Seat of our wisdom
Cause of our joy
Mystical Rose
Franchot Tone
Rita Gam
Talullah Bankhead
José Ferrer
Betsy von Furstenberg

O Betsy von Furstenberg, with your unpronounceable name and your upturned nose! The nights I spend in bed pushing up my blunt-humped little nose with my finger so it'll turn up and say peek-a-boo like yours. O Betsy, how I'd love a name and a nose like yours. Ever conscious of her brogue, Mammie practices enunciating these names as she kneels, step by step, polishing the brass guards on the stairs.

As Mammie's passion with names grows, my passion for Miss D.'s house takes flight. There isn't a chair I don't want to sit in, a window I don't want to look out, or a stairway I don't want to make an entrance on. But I have to be quiet. Though Miss D. doesn't actually say it, she's uncomfortable around children. She is. Even around me, with my airs. Silent as a ghost, polite as a princess, I am still a child. I want to be Queen of the Castle. If all Mammie wants is to buy a house in Astoria, all I want is this one.

When I cast my eyes back, East Fifty-fifth Street between Park and Lexington Avenues looks like a fifties *New Yorker* cover. It's autumn. The Central Synagogue on the corner is lit up. The flagstone sidewalk is damp and gray. I'm wearing my navy uniform and beanie, which announces that I am a student of Immaculate Conception School, or "the Mac," as we call it. My jumper breast pocket holds an ironed handkerchief with yellow roses, a Miss D. castoff. The voluptuousness of the cloth, squeezed into the tiny pocket, makes me look one breasted. Like an Amazon.

I've galloped in. I can make it in twenty minutes from school to town house. I've stopped at Gristede's for Mammie. Beef for stew. She'll cook it up for Miss D. And I'll eat some, too. With tomatoes and peas. Frozen Bird's Eye peas, mind. Definitely not Irish.

I walk on the opposite side of the street so I can take in the blue-and-white ceramic cartouche of a bowl of flowers over the front door. I open the door and eye the ivy and latticework wallpaper in the hall. I note the names of Miss D.'s tenants on the doorbells. Gloria Safier: "The Agent," Mammie says reverentially. Joe Dexter, who uses the nom de plume Cholly Knickerbocker in the *Journal American*. Mammie's thrilled to bits to have a nodding acquaintance with a columnist we gobble up. "Jolly" Knickerbocker is how she says it. She's never corrected.

I put on an apron over my uniform and sit on a kitchen stool waiting for my can of Bumble Bee and cup of tea. Mammie never sits. I check to see if there's a *Playbill* to look at. Yet there's no time for lollygagging. I've ice trays to empty and cigarette boxes to fill. And I must do them fast. We've got to get back to Astoria to cook Carey's dinner on time, or risk a night of darkness.

It's a pleasure to keep Miss D.'s three floors sparkling. I have tasks on each that I perform without question. After tea, I head for the living room, step stool in one hand, rag in the other. Over the marble mantel is an oil painting of a snowy Eiffel Tower by Utrillo. I keep a notebook. And I write down "you trill oh" so I remember how to pronounce it. After feather-dusting the frame, I turn my attention to my objects of desire: Miss D.'s troop of china cats who preside over the mantel.

"Now, Alice M'rie, don't rearrange the cats. Miss D. likes them the way they are."

Ha! I think, 'tis I who arranged them in the first place.

Presiding in the corner is Shamrocks. His emerald rhinestone eyes are the size of sour balls. He's nearly as big as Mitzi. Miss D. says he's her lucky cat. Next to him is a gray kitten playing with his tail. He's from Georg Jensen, who I thought was one of Miss D.'s poker pals, till the boys in Miss D.'s office up on the third floor set me straight. Next to him is a striped kitten batting a ball. And next to him, a bright blue cat with orange whiskers in a hissing position, who's lead-heavy. He stays where he is.

Sooner or later Miss D. will give Shamrocks to me. I know she will. Or one of the other cats. She knows I love cats. She knows about Mitzi. Surely she doesn't need them all. She wouldn't even miss one. She gets stuff all the time. Like the dolly up in her bedroom. The dolly with the white flannel dress, little straw hat, and the blue china eyes. Maybe she'll give her to me if . . .

If I'm silent.

If I empty my ice trays without knocking the cubes on the floor.

If I don't clomp my shoes as I walk.

If I stay quietly away out of sight when Gloria Vanderbilt, Zachary Scott, or Paula Laurence come by.

When Columbus Day rolls round, it's my job to change the slipcovers from the yellow and gray stripes of summer to the Prussian blue frolicking shepherds and shepherdesses of winter. Once I asked Mammie if she frolicked like this when she was a girl in Ireland. She said no.

In the mahogany-red and silver dining room, there are cigarette boxes to fill with Chesterfields. Match strikers to fill with English matches. Ivory candles to put in candelabras. When Philip de Witt Ginder, Miss D.'s husband, who served in World War II and the Korean War ("the General," we call him), is around and not stationed on Governors Island, Mammie says I must curtsy to him.

"Good morning, sir General."

"Good morning, Little Alice."

I salute and curtsy at the same time.

The dining room is presided over by a nude portrait of Miss D.'s back and bum, in a blue that matches the slipcovers. Bold is what it is. A "near occasion of sin." Avert your eyes. But I peek. It's interesting. When I have my portrait painted, I'll not have me in blue.

Peeks turn to looks. I confess my "near occasion" to Father Lyons.

"Where did you see this portrait, my child?"

"In *Life* magazine." What could I say? I dust a nude picture of the lady who owns the house where my mammie works?

And that's only the first floor. It's nothing compared to Miss D.'s bedroom, the sanctum sanctorum sorely coveted by me, where I'm not allowed in unless summoned. In its mystery, it's as inviting as Titania's fairy bower was to Bottom. Tints of gray, pink, and baby blue melt one to the other, gliding in flowery sprigged glory from wallpaper to chaise to the big, big bed, its silken coverlet proclaiming *JD*.

If there's no school, I come in with Mammie and get a glimpse of the bedroom through the ritual of Miss D.'s breakfast. At 9:20 Mammie and I ascend the kitchen stairs with a wicker breakfast tray, covered in white linen, containing an offering of Earl Grey tea and wheat toast with the crusts cut off. A small blue pitcher of Golden Blossom honey and fresh-squeezed, mind, grapefruit juice.

Tucked under my arm are the *New York Times*, *Variety*, and the *Hollywood Reporter*. Miss D.'s still asleep. Rolled to her side. Head to the phone. Nightgown on. Peignoir thrown asunder. Her mink, a crushed gardenia still pinned to it, tossed on the chaise.

"Lovely day, Miss D.," says Mammie, blocking my presence.

Can't let the *chisler* (Irish slang for "kids") frighten Miss D. so early in the morning. Miss D. says nothing. I take a slow walk 'round the bed so I can torture her with my presence. Think I'm going to break something, do you? Huh? Huh? 'Tis I'm the guardian of your cats.

I take it all in. Drink it up, furtively, silently. I'll dream about this for days. Me in that bed, all dolled up in a fluffy bed jacket. Surrounded by bookcases crammed

with bestsellers and scripts. Piles of *Playbill*. Flowers. A
jug of finely sharpened pencils. Little vases with pink
rosebuds. A push-button phone. An air conditioner.
Music boxes with angels, playing little gold instruments.
And dolls. Dolls everywhere. Stuffed animals, too.

Oh . . . the dolly of my dreams has been moved to
the chair. She's not on the chaise. Maybe Miss D.'s been
playing with her. Mammie says all these are gifts, mind,
from admirers. (Carey calls them "phonies.") Admirers
who love Jean Dalrymple, Jean, Jeanie, JD—or to Mammie
and me, Miss D.

I put the papers down and head down the hall for
the bathroom to do my morning job. In passing I give a
wave to the boys in the office. I'm trusted in the bathroom,
with its cabbage rose wallpaper and framed photograph of
a white cat with a green eye and a blue eye. Even my Mitzi
doesn't match this cat's splendor. Every Elizabeth Arden
elixir known to woman stands awaiting the touch of Miss
D. Awaiting my touch is the round-as-a-moon mirror, its
radiance in disarray from a dusting of face powder the night
before. I can hear Mammie and Miss D. in the bedroom.

"John Gambling"—the newscaster—"says it might
shower. Should I call a car?"

From a cabinet I take a can of Glass Wax and a
rag. I climb up on the marble vanity, careful not to tinkle
the crystal sconces that frame the mirror. I spread a layer
of wax smoothly, carefully, evenly, on this wonderful
mirror and wait for it to dry. Miss D. is talking about a

dress Mammie's got to return to Bergdorf's. The mirror whitens dry. I take my index finger and carefully, neatly, classily sign my autograph.

Alice Marie Carey
Alice Marie Carey
Alice M'r . . .

"I KNOW ALL ABOUT THAT," says Geoffrey as we pull into the parking area of Bantry House, "but should we buy this house?"

We should. We must. I must bring Mammie back to Ireland in the grandeur she craved. From Dublin airport, I call the agent and propose £33,000.

"Ee'ra," says he, "ee'll spoil the shite fr' th' tar." I have no idea what he means. I go up a thousand and the place is ours for £34,000.

And a small cabin
build there

BUYING A HOUSE IN IRELAND separated our New York friends into wheat and chaff. At best when we announced our news, we could see their eyes glaze over. Then little wispy smiles crinkled their mouths. At worst there were interrogations. Everyone asked the same questions in the same order, with the same intensity and the same frequency. I thought of making up flyers with questions and answers.

Geoffrey and I bought a house in Ireland.
#1—*Ohhhhh . . . where?*
Cork.
(INQUIRING FACE GOES BLANK.)
Where??
LESSON LEARNED: Dublin is Ireland. Ireland is Dublin. No one has heard of Cork.

#2—*How long does it take to get there?*
Five hours . . . same as to L.A.
(INQUIRING EYES WIDEN AND MOUTH DROPS OPEN.)
LESSON LEARNED: Flying over the U.S.A. is one thing, over the Atlantic another.

#3—But is it safe . . . there?
It's safe.
(INQUIRING FACE TAKES ON A PAINED EXPRESSION.)
LESSON LEARNED: People think the violence in the North is all over Ireland.

#4—How often will you get over there?
We don't know.
(INQUIRING FACE BECOMES A PITYING FACE.)
LESSON LEARNED: People want to know where you are and what you are doing.

Questioning over, Face assumes a concerned expression that turns into a beaming smile. When I ask why, they say, "Oh . . . I've always wanted to go to Ireland." Yet when I meet the same person on the street a week later, and they ask me the same set of questions, with the same intensity, it's as if the first conversation never took place.

It was worse on Fire Island. Neighbors took our move as a rejection of the community and themselves. In a place where the first words you hear getting off the ferry are "Welcome home," our impending move implied that Geoffrey and I no longer considered Cherry Grove our home. People couldn't believe we were leaving. "After how many years? . . . *No!*" No matter how often people demanded *why*, and no matter how often I tried to explain *why*, friends talked with friends who talked with other friends, and they all made up answers to suit themselves.

Geoffrey and Alice are moving to Ireland because:

They've abandoned New York.

They hate Fire Island.

They're retiring.

They're opening a bed-and-breakfast.

They can live there tax-free.

She's a secret member of the IRA.

They're very rich.

Not a one is true.

When interrogation turns to architecture, I'm at my best. Oh, I say, trying to get them to laugh, we bought a ruin. "*A ruin?*" Inquiring Face looks interested.

"That's real-estate lingo," I say. "Do you want a bungalow or a ruin?"

Depending how up on *Architectural Digest* the inquisitor is, conversation can bloom or wither. Movies are to blame, *The Quiet Man* especially. People want Ireland to be quaint, thatched, oil lamp'ed, leprechaun'ed, Guinness'ed, and green. I tell them, "It's green all right. Greener than that long shot of Emerald City. But Ireland has problems: poverty, drugs, people on the dole living in projects, the middle class living in bungalows plopped by the side of the road. It's just like America." Wrong tack, Alice. Yer average Joe is not interested in truth. Stick with Maureen O'Hara gathering her sheep.

"Bungalow" shocks. Inquiring Face, clutching a copy of *Travel & Leisure*, looks stricken.

"This is modern Ireland," I say. "Young couples want starter homes with all 'mod cons.'"

But I lose them again. Inquiring Eyes glaze over at the idea of the Irish wanting something so philistine as convenience. What brings them right back is if I say "Our ruin looks like something out of *Masterpiece Theatre*." With that, Eyes sparkle so brightly I see them merging *Brideshead Revisited, The Mill on the Floss, Mapp & Lucia, and The Irish R.M.* into a dancing, shimmering collage of style, taste, and class, starring Geoffrey and me as lord and lady of the Manor.

Then I pull out the stops and invoke my one word of clout: *Georgian.*

"Geoffrey and I bought a ruined nineteenth-century Georgian farmhouse."

"Ahhhh . . ."

Harmony is restored among the style queens who are our friends. Everyone believes they know what a Georgian farmhouse looks like. They hear *farm*, picture *barn*, and start imagining a large, red *American* barn, with a crystal chandelier swinging from the ceiling. Because of this style confusion, I stopped using *farm*; yet Geoffrey persisted. He thought *farm* would make us and the property seem less pretentious.

I found myself downplaying the house, emphasizing Ireland's landscape and history: "It's nothing fancy. These houses are all over Ireland. No, it's not a listed building. We reckon the Big House was probably built for an English land agent during the Famine. The ruined cottages were probably those of evicted Catholics during this time. The whole shebang comes as a package. And it's on three acres."

Famine shuts them up. *Acre* stuns them. Most of our New York City friends haven't a clue how big an acre is.

IF I EVER TAKE UP NEEDLEPOINT, this is what I'll stitch on a cushion: "Buying a ruin is one thing, restoring it another."

Just because the Irish speak English doesn't mean we understand them, nor they us. Rules are different here. Everything is different. We need a doctorate in Irish Bureaucracy. Customs, stamp tax, building permits, V.A.T., auctioneer, debit, right of way, the unexplained initials of F.R.I.C.S., F.S.C.S., M.I.A.V.A. And *The* Architect and *The* Builder, always said in hallowed tone.

The worst of the lot is "holiday home." Because we have a New York residence, our ruin is called a holiday home. This piece of vernacular doesn't discriminate between our brimming-with-potential wreck, a meticulously restored castle, and a dreary unpainted bungalow with plastic windows.

The quid pro quo of owning a *perceived* holiday home means every time we are in Ireland, we are on holiday. Take my butcher in Bantry. The first thing out of Paddy's mouth when I'm in the door is "Over again on holiday?" Never mind the mud, the cow shite on my boots, the bleary look in my eye, and the dirt on my Barbour, the all-purpose wax coat I've traded in my black stuff for. If I'm in Bantry, I'm on holiday.

"Paddy," I say, "I'll tell you what a holiday is. A holiday is when I summon a waiter and say, 'I'll have a whiskey sour please.' That's a holiday."

When Geoffrey and I trooped out to Fire Island every weekend, we weren't on holiday and neither were our neighbors. It was simply what all our friends did as part of their week. It was routine. But let us get on a plane and cross the Atlantic, then we're on holiday. It would be easier if I simply played along and said, "Oh yes, Geoffrey and I love having a holiday home. Ireland is great fun. It's so green and restful. We never even need to sit down."

Yet the sitting part is true. For well over the year that it took to get planning permission to restore the buildings, we never once sat down in the Big House. Of course, we had no place to sit, but that's no excuse. We thought of buying a few old chairs but didn't. Standing became the norm. We'd be well back in New York when it would hit us that once again we never had sat down. This dynamic changed somewhat with our first purchase, an Edwardian toilet, labeled "The Maxim," which we bought in a salvage yard. It sat around for two years before being installed, and we occasionally took a breather on it.

Years ago when I was acting, I appeared in Al Carmines's musicals at Judson Memorial Church, in

Greenwich Village. Al, a Baptist minister, occasionally rounded up the cast to ask us to express our "concerns." At the time, I never once raised my hand. Concerns? Irish Catholics have far more than concern. We have fear. However, now that I'm here in Ireland, I do have a few concerns.

My biggest concern is shite. *Shite!* I tell you. (Pronounce the long *i*. The Irish don't say "shit.") Picture yourself flying over Ireland. Look at the fields! Aren't they green! A veritable patchwork quilt of emerald-chartreuse-apple-green-pea-blue-hunter-seaweed-sage-tea grass. Yet cleverly concealed in the lovely green fields are large steaming piles of cow patties, as Mammie'd say. Shite, I say. Our three unfenced acres are brimming with it.

And so we give thanks for the dung beetle. Say you're out in the fields for a stroll, stepping over great shimmering masses of cow pat here . . . here . . . over there, too. Then a few days later, you notice there . . . there by the hawthorn tree, the shite is gone and all is lovely and green again. Well, you can credit the dung beetles, who just love cow pat. They work overtime to please. Though perhaps not on the day the mud sucked me down into a great oozy pile of the stuff, and my wellie'd feet were the only dry spot. Which brings me to a fashion concern, if not a bona fide fashion tip.

A few years ago *W* magazine ran a small picture of Princess Diana's legs clad in pea-green boots. Aha! I thought, those are the boots for me. On a trip to London

I went to Hardy's, where the salesman told me sincerely that these boots would keep my feet "quite dry in the field."

"Ah, sir," said I, "these boots will never see a field. I'm going to wear them as rain boots in New York."

As it turns out, that Hardy's salesman was right, if not psychic, for I'm now wearing these boots in the ever-wet fields of Ireland.

The week Geoffrey and I returned to Ireland to interview architects, it pissed rain for three days straight. But our zeal was unbounded. And we were fortified by a winter's perusal of shelter magazines.

There wasn't a book on Irish houses, grand or artisan, English cottages, thatched or timbered, Scottish lodges, cairn or castle, or Welsh farmhouses that we hadn't bought and scoured for ideas. Old college paperbacks, their pages yellow with age, were tossed into the bin to make room for Hugh Lander's *House Restorer's Guide*, *Collins Complete Home Restoration Manual*, *Irish Countryside Buildings*, *The Perfect Country Cottage*, *A Lost Tradition*, *Celtic Style*, *English Style*, *Classic Country Style*, and more.

Now we were lit, loaded, and ready to go find our own McKim, Mead & White. He would be an Irish man of vision, for there were no female architects in our area. Most of all he would be sensitive. Articulate. Imaginative. Someone who loved old houses. Someone who saw what we saw, and wouldn't bollix the good design already there.

We'd occasionally ask ourselves why did we even need an architect? The Big House had sat on that ridge unattended for years. Even in the rain, it's beautiful. But it's uninhabitable. And we hadn't a clue how to install electricity, plumbing, phone lines. Establish boundaries, erect cow-proof, sheep-proof, bull-proof fencing. Much less dig a foundation, put in a damp-proof course, lay drainage pipes, build windows, match roof tiles, trusses, and floorboards. That's why we needed an architect.

For three storm-tossed days we plodded around in the mud, interviewing architects. One wore a gray suit, one a blue, one had a raincoat. None carried an umbrella or wore wellies. I called them our three little maids from school.

I kept trying to lighten the situation for myself, and shut out Carey's mocking voice playing in my head. "Ee'ra, th' two've need an architect, all right. I'll give ye architect. Phony leeches, they are. Just like th' two've."

The three men with wet hair had a lot to say about our ruin. They jumped on the old planked wood floor upstairs. Oh, it's very solid. One used a teeny-tiny meter to measure the rising damp. Of course, it's still pissing a blue streak outside. Oh, it's damp here . . . here . . . and here . . . but you got a "sun trap" in the back there. And they'd point to the swampy land at the rear of the house. They watched rain course down the hill. Now, there's the place for the percolation field. They admired the fire-places, the size of the windows, the stone work, and the cove ceilings. Oh, there was big money here once. It has detail, pretension even. So much for my downplaying this house on Fire Island.

As the consultation wound up, the architects said either "I've seen this old house up there in the trees for years" or "I've been driving by here for years and never noticed the place." What they didn't say (as they pulled their suit collars up to their ears) is: You must be daft to buy it.

The unrelenting rain had us delirious. We hadn't sat down for hours, nor eaten. As we drove back to Bantry House, with its roaring fire and hot toddies, we realized that it's one thing to buy an old house like this, and it's quite another to have the money to restore it. But we came over to choose an architect, and choose one we did. We chose the one who brought his dog along, and knew the Latin names of the trees in the front of the house.

Back in New York, death intervened, grabbed us by the scruff of the neck, and said: *Wait a minute, you think you can lose me by returning to the olde sod?*

Well, you won't.

Scott is going to die.

Storms will ravage Fire Island.

And Scott did die. Barely forty. He had been Geoffrey's gym buddy. As Scott's lover, Jack, had been before him. And Scott and Jack were not the first.

Fire Island had become a metaphor for death. In August 1995 a hurricane stalled offshore, destroying houses, dunes, and beach. That winter an ice storm crumbled five houses all in a row. In a flash, they rolled into the sea and sank. I was on the phone with a friend as he was watching the house next door go down.

The subzero winter sent deer deeper into the communities in search of food. At Magic Flute, they devoured 463 newly planted spring bulbs, along with the lilac buds, hydrangea buds, our beautiful rhododendron (the tallest one in the Grove) and her sister Sappho the Smaller, of the lush red blossom.

Yeats wrote, "Too long a sacrifice can make a stone of the heart." My heart was in danger of this. Geoffrey's too. Crusty, old scabby scars prevented me from crying when the phone would ring and I'd hear so-and-so had finally died. *Finally! Finally!* AIDS does that.

In 1991, when Geoffrey was working for the Gay Men's Health Crisis (GMHC) as their Director of Communications and I was a volunteer, I kept a list of everyone I knew who had died of AIDS. There were 107 men and one child. Then I stopped counting. And crying. By the time Scott died, on March 1, 1996—St. David's Day, during a blizzard—I had no more tears to shed.

In the midst of going back and forth to the hospital to see Scott, Geoffrey and I decided in a flash of clarity that at this point we simply could not do justice to the Big House. It would be too much for us to handle. Though the architect had drawn up plans, revised them, and drawn up new plans again, we reckoned it would be better to cut our teeth on the ruined cottages.

We would restore the "long house," as we began to call the stable, as a dress rehearsal for the Big House.

When Scott died we gave up our idea of returning to the cottage to muck it out. Instead I cleaned out Scott's apartment. As I packed up his clothes, I thought about Cherry Grove.

It's still so beautiful, but there's not a house untouched by death. The Japanese House is not the same without Gordon—the barges of soil he'd bring over for his vegetable garden. And Eric's Shocking Poverty. How he built that long deck so Tommy Tune could dance on it. Waine's sign still says FAIRIES AT THE BOTTOM OF THE GARDEN, but lesbians live there now. New owners destroyed David Baker's English garden, all those pink irises we gave him after his production of *Candide*. Martin's garden is gone, too. How could those idiots take down the red ramp his wisteria clung to?

I found myself dwelling on the wrong of what *was*, hoping it would give validation for the right of what was to be: our selling Magic Flute and moving on.

And what would Scott say?

He'd say, "Go for it, girl!"

On my fourth can of Classic Coke, the nasties would creep in.

Mean little tears blurred my eyes.

I'm mad at Scott for dying.

I'm mad at everyone else for dying and leaving Geoffrey and me alone.

49

I'm mad at the Grove for not being what it once was.

I'm mad at the new people who came in, bought the old houses, and never asked or cared about who once lived there.

I'm mad at myself for longing for the old days.

Yet Cherry Grove was the only place I ever felt at home. Straight people thought it strange. I could see it in their eyes. When I was asked which community Geoffrey and I lived in on Fire Island, I'd say Cherry Grove. Then I'd see them giving me the once-over. People know that the Grove is a gay community, so they'd think, What's a straight woman doing there? Is she a dyke? And if she is, what's she doing with him? Then they'd look at Geoffrey and wonder whether he was gay.

Yet when I cast my eyes back and see me running in from school to help out Mammie at Miss D.'s, I see myself running toward Homer Poupart, one of the office boys. He was Miss D.'s self-appointed majordomo. When my tasks were finished and I had nothing left to do, I'd climb up the back stairs to my playground—Jean Dalrymple's office. My playmates were her office boys—"the lads," as they were called.

Their room was across the hall from Miss D.'s bedroom. It had the coldest air conditioner in the world. The men were all bachelors. That's what Mammie called them. I didn't know they were gay. All I knew was they loved me.

It's a Thursday in August. Miss D. has already left for her house in the country. On the dot of two, Homer parades down the kitchen stairs wearing a pink candy-stripe shirt, a violet pussycat bow tie, and red suspenders. His graying hair parts floppily in the middle. His teeth buck. Before we see him, we hear him singing.

Here we are, Christopher Street,
I live in the heart of Greenwich Village.
Life is Gayyyyyyyy! Life is sweet.

Every line a step, every step a gesture. Homer's here for tuna 'n' toast.

"Big Alice, get that kettle going! Attention, Mr. and Mrs. America and all the ships at sea. Flash! Flash!"

With his buck teeth Mammie's name comes out "Big Alisssshhh."

"They're un-dreary-ing Susie and smacking her right up against Richard Burton in a romance *du coeur* called *Time Remembered*. I said, 'Susie, get out of that flannel nightgown and put Anne to bed.' [Susan Strasberg starred in *The Diary of Anne Frank* on Broadway.] Alice dwa-ling, have you read her diary?"

"I've my own diary."

"Big Alice, get Doubleday on the phone immediately! Little Alice must read Anne Frank's diary. And Virginia Woolf's . . . and Cecil Beaton's. Someday I'll tell you what Cecil said to me, and where. You know what they say about mad dogs and Englishmen?"

"Mammie, don't. I'll get them from the library."

"Furthermore"—tuna's sputtering from his mouth—"she'll costar with Helen! I said to Miss D.,

51

'Helen should get the hell out of Nyack and back to Broadway.'"

"Helen who?" says Mammie.

"Helen Hayes! Big Alice, I'm shocked. Miss Hayes is as holy as the BVM. You must devise a set of theater flash cards for Little Alice: Roz—Russell. Noely and Coely—Noël and Cole. Sexy Rexy—Harrison. And so on.

"Vernon Duke's doing the incidental music. Miles White is doing the costumes. Big Alice, this tuna is delish! If you've another smidgen . . . ?"

Mammie gets on the phone to Gristede's. "Joe, we need a Golden Blossom, four Bumble Bees, and a brown Arnold."

"Albert Marre's staging. He'll do for Susie what he did for Betsy in *The Chalk Garden*. Then again, Betsy had Beaton for the costumes. Hmmmm . . . Big Alice, you have a way with tuna."

Lunch over, Homer returns to the men's room (as Mammie calls it), picking his teeth with the special goose quills he gets at Caswell-Massey.

WE'RE WASHING MINT JULEP GLASSES.

"O Mammie, Homer's a sketch. He always wears pink and he lives in Greenwich Village. Where's that?"

"Downtown."

Mammie blasts hot water on glasses so narrow, my hand can barely fit inside.

"Would you spell that now?" And she does.

"That's Green-witch."

Mammie sniffs. "Oh, he's a great one, Homer is, with his pink shirts."

Homer calls down the banister, "Little Alice dwa-ling, when you're through, come up for a confab."

I wash. I scrub. I'm fast as a flea. I shut up about how much I love these glasses decorated with pink ele-phants and zebras riding a merry-go-round, ones that Miss D. never uses. And I'm thrilled to bits to be sum-moned to the men's room on this hot afternoon.

"Don't o'erstay yer welcome, Alice M'rie."

I trot up the kitchen stairs to the office. It's as gray as a battleship, as brown as a Camel. The lads are huddled at their desks, surrounded by a nimbus of smoke. There's John Fernley, with that glass eye of his scaring the daylights out of me. I'd rather be blind with a dog and a stick.

"Is it in straight?" he asks Homer, who says, "Yes, dwa-ling."

But it isn't; it's crooked. I can't look at him. I'll look at David Powers. He's blond and cute. Hello, David. Hello, Miss Alice.

Homer's at his desk. The nice one. The one in front of the air conditioner.

"Little Alice, come over here and let me cool your brow. As I was explaining to my fellow travelers, we need an extra pair of eyes to complete our survey."

"We need more than that," snorts Michael Shurtluff. "We need an escape plan."

"Ignore her," says Homer.

Her? A man as smart as Homer should know his pronouns.

"Little Alice, forget what the good nuns teach you. The Bible was written by Daniel Blum." Homer points to a shelf of books with dust jackets in Crayola colors.

"These sacred volumes are *the* Daniel Blum *Theatre World*. Each volume represents a year in the theater. What plays were done. Who was in them. Who produced. Who directed. Who starred. Miss D. is throughout."

He takes down Volume 2, hands it to me, and I read:

Dalrymple, Jean. Producer. Publicity Director.
Born September 2, 1910, in Morristown, N.J.
Is divorced from critic Ward Morehouse.
Started in vaudeville.

"We don't mention vaudeville to Miss D. anymore."

"Now, dwa-ling, I'll make you a list of names. When you take a break from scrubbing the kitchen and making ice cubes, come up here and look them up. Write down what shows they were in, the year, the director, etc., etc., etc., as Yul Brynner says. He's your first name."

I write down *Yule* Brynner.

"I guarantee by the time you're my age, you'll have spent more time with Daniel Blum than with Jesus."

Later, when Mammie and I are going home on the subway, I study my list.

"Homer says his name is spelled Y-u-l, not Y-u-l-e." I put my hand on my hip and stick out my teeth. "'Alish dwa-ling, shave one, burn the other.' Isn't that a scream? Shave one. Burn the other."

Mammie's deep into Walter Winchell. "Alice M'rie, don't ye be imitating people. Ladies don't do that."

"Guess what Homer sang to the boys as they were collating scripts? 'I like a boy in June. How about you? I like a Gershwin tune. . . .' Gotta put him on my list. 'How about you?' Homer's so cute; I just love him. He says we must visit him in his pee-a-da-tear in the Village."

Ditmars Boulevard. Last stop.

On to Horn & Hardart to pick up Carey's favorites, baked beans and custard. Then to Deutsch Brothers for pork steaks.

"Homer says when he was a monk he ate no meat."

"Alice M'rie, believe ye me, Homer was no monk."

"Is Homer married, then?"

"Not at all."

"Isn't he lonely?"

"Why would he be lonely?"

"Does he have a girlfriend?"

"None that I know of."

"Homer says the Village is full of artistes. I want to bean artiste when I grow up so I can live in there, too." Mammie scratches her forehead.

"Joe, I want pork steaks and a silver-tip roast beef for the weekend."

"Mrs. Denis, you're looking fine this hot evening."

I watch Joe eviscerate a fresh chicken, guts and all.

"Mammie, if Homer had a girlfriend, he'd not have to eat out at night because she'd cook for him. Right? We must get him a girlfriend."

We walk home in dead silence. Mammie's tired. Carey should help out more. Thinks he's killing himself if he picks up a quart of milk. Slaves're what we are. That what Mammie says. We're approaching the house. We see Carey's bald head hanging out the window hoping to catch a breeze. It's roasting. We've no air conditioner. Not even a fan. Carey says it'd give him a wheeze.

Mammie has her key in the door. I'm still banging my drum.

"But why doesn't Homer have a girlfriend? Doesn't he want one?" Mammie stops, takes the key out of the door, puts the pork steaks down on the stoop, and looks at me very calmly.

"Alice M'rie, Homer likes men. That's why he doesn't have a girlfriend."

I'M NOW HOMER'S GIRLFRIEND. He's changed my life. He knows every song ever written and sings them all for me. We'll have Manhattan, the Bronx, and Staten Island, too . . .

when June is busting out all over . . . we can walk down the avenue . . . with cocktails for two.

Our tuna lunches are legend. Legend, I tell you. The other lads want to join in, but Homer squeezes Mammie and persuades her to keep it exclusive "in our little den of iniquity." He even brings records from home. And we sing along with them. All this when Miss D.'s in the country, of course.

I've a new trick. Before I go out to Gristede's, and if Mammie's not looking, I pop into Miss D.'s bathroom for a swipe of mascara. Helena Rubenstein Jewish mascara. Homer says *Cleopatra* started the craze. There's not an eye that can't benefit from it, he says. But it's so heavy. My upper lash falls into my lower. I'm half blind with beauty. Homer says true beauty comes through tea and prayer. I'm laughing my head off. He says he's down on his knees praying every night. John Fernley's eye pops out with the laughing.

It's a Friday evening. The lads're gone. Homer's going to a place on an island called Cherry Grove. He says people dance the night away and cherry trees grow right on the beach. I'm up here tidying the office.

The air conditioner's freezing the place. Oh, the glamour of it all. Ashtrays heaped with butts. Smoke hanging in the icy air. And yes, it is . . . just a lingering hint of Homer's cologne. Canoe. Not pronounced like the boat. I sit at his desk and survey his world.

Ringg. Ringg. Yes? Yes—oh, Miss Kelly . . . of course I'll call you Grace. . . . I'm deeply honored to be your bridesmaid. And my mammie? . . . Yes, she'd love to be one. Thank you. The pleasure's all mine. . . . Oh, we'd love to travel first class.

This is a room of glamour. Real glamour. Not just in wallpaper or furniture, but in books. Walls of books. Every single script Studio Duplicating ever duplicated. Every issue of *Life* published by Mr. Luce. Every issue of *Look*, stacked neatly by me. Every single *Playbill* of every play Miss D. ever saw. Thousands of them. And my Bible, *Theatre World*. The boys never put them in order. Yellow for 1951 to 1952. Purple for 1952 to 1953. Orange for 1956 to 1957.

The purple's my new favorite. There's the Catholic, Elaine Stritch. Boy, could she use a little mascara. She's wearing dotted Swiss in a full skirt. Her mouth's open. She must be singing. Mammie and I saw her getting into an elevator at Best & Co., tweed suit, spindly legs, and looking like she was going to fall over. Maybe she's lapsed.

Move on to my current favorite, *Wish You Were Here*. Lads running around with their shirts off . . .

Daniel Blum says: "*Wish You Were Here* takes place at Camp Karefree, a summer camp for adults, where friendships are formed to last a whole life through."

Can't imagine a bunch of grown-ups in camp.

I search the cast list for familiar names, names I may have gotten off Miss D.'s Christmas cards. Here's

Jack Cassidy on a bike. He and his wife, Shirley Jones, did *The Beggar's Opera* for Miss D. Mammie won't let me ride a bike. She says I'll brain myself. There's Rain Winslow, Orson Bean's new wife. Saw them downstairs waiting for Miss D. She's having a baby and he was hugging her and hugging her and rubbing her belly. Don't want to see that. Ooooh, there's the blondie—Sheila Bond, playing a girl named Fay. No saint's name that. Must be Jewish. I'd like to be Jewish. Then I could jig around like her with the lads in shorts and not be in sin.

"Alice M'rie . . . what're ye doing up there?"

"I'm dusting and emptying the ashtrays."

"When ye're done, come down and do the mirror in the small room."

I hide my favorite *Theatre World* under my cardigan, go downstairs, and take it into my favorite room, Miss. D.'s mirrored little nook off the living room with the mink-coated daybed. When I finish dusting, I'll look at the goddess of Volume 7. Carol Channing. I love her to bits.

Carol's in a musical called *Gentlemen Prefer Blondes*. Every year she sends Miss D. the best Christmas card. She and her husband and son actually have their picture taken and put on a card. No drawings of the shivering virgin mucking around in the manger for them. I always put it at the front of the mantel.

O Carol, with your short blondie hair, your big teeth, big lips, and big gestures. When I grow up I want to look just like you.

Daniel says: "*Gentlemen Prefer Blondes* is a musical comedy in two acts and twelve scenes about adventures in gold digging by the fabulous Lorelei Lee."

I want to be Carol Channing. I stand and look at myself in the mirror. Take off my beanie. Plump up that hankie. No. Makes me look lopsided. Get a rubber band. Skim the hair off my face. Show some cheekbone. There. That's it!

Ta-da! And now 110 East Fifty-fifth presents its very own little Lorelei Lee. In the fractured mirror there are many Alice M'ries. Many Lorelei Lees. Eyes wide. Teeth apart. Left arm up to heaven. Pretend I'm waving someone off. Top deck of the *Île de France*. Right leg slantylike. Ignore my socks. That's it. Smile. Oh, they're calling me darling. Hello, darling. Dazzle them.

"Alice M'rie, come down for the tea."

"Right."

Of clay and wattles made

WE RENTED OUT MAGIC FLUTE for the summer. This freed us up to go over to Ireland on Memorial Day weekend to meet on-site with the architect, his assistant, and the builder. From our first look at the house that Thanksgiving, it took one year and five and a half months to get to May 15, 1996, the day work began on the stables.

Our neighbors, the Johnstons, said that cars were practically careening into the ditch at the sight of the changes happening up on the ridge. Foxes were seen marching toward Schull, in search of another ridge to hang their hats. Even the fairies were reported to be boarding up their mossy windows in preparation for a visit from the god Chaos.

As Geoffrey and I drove up the laneway to the stables, we were greeted by the Seven Dwarves of Restoration: Happy, Reluctant, Fearful, Suspicious, Wary, Hopeful, and Doubtful. But Chaos reigned. There wasn't a worker in sight. And there wasn't a scintilla of charm left to our ruin.

In front of the stables, softened somewhat by May-flowering horse chestnut trees, were a digger, an electric generator, a cement mixer, bags and bags marked

"Irish cement," piles of stone taken from the building, and a pile of sand as tall as a pyramid. Rolls of plastic sheeting, rolls of yolk-yellow plastic drainage pipes, buttercup-yellow rolls of insulation, neatly stacked blue Bangor slates, and stuff. More stuff than was used to build this building in the first place.

Floating down from the Big House came the drone of Gay Byrne's voice. We knew what was up. It was eleven o'clock. Our team was having their elevenses in the canteen they set up in the scullery.

Tea boiled away on a hot plate that was hooked up to an electric generator outside in the yard. A small fire fed by twigs and Fig Newton wrappers glowed in the fireplace. Tins of biscuits, a quart of milk, a full pound box of Barry's tea, and a three-pound sack of sugar sat on the mantel next to a jar of Old Time marmalade, depicting a hearth and cat. Mugs and cigarettes littered an old pine table neatly covered with sheets of the *Independent*. Sitting around the table, on plastic milk crates culled from the supermarket, were Johnnie K. (the builder), along with his helpers, the architect, and the architect's site supervisor—all of them having a cuppa.

And there were Geoffrey and myself wearing our New York black, stepping into this "Oi-rish" situation. Lord and lady of the manor. The blow-ins with money to burn.

"Would 'ee like a drop?" asks Johnnie K., indicating a bottle of Paddy on the mantel. Geoffrey, I thought to myself, this is Ireland.

That it was the feast of St. Dymphna, patroness of the insane, seemed appropriate. For not only were Geoffrey and I not needed, we seemed to be held in contempt (in an Irish, charming way, of course) by the architect and site supervisor, whom I began to think of as Dog and Dog's Body. From the architect's perspective, our decision to put the Big House on hold and deal first with the most ruinous Ruin lost us credibility as serious house restorers. It also lost them money, since converting the stables would cost less.

Worse, the property no longer seemed ours. It was the builder's. For three days we walked around, and walked around, and walked around, checking on things. Yet there was only so much attention we could give Johnnie K. and the lads as they dug out three feet of earth in the stables in preparation for laying down the damp-proof course and a layer of cement for the foundation of the floor. We missed seeing the salvaged roof slates being laid down on top of that. By that time, we were back in New York.

Our main job was making payments to "Mr. Cash," as he's called in Ireland, cash payment being a method not only customary, but also preferred. The Irish way of banking is as casual as the New York way is rigid. We were never asked for identification in a bank. That we possessed a checkbook and *said* we were Alice Carey and Geoffrey Knox was enough for the teller. We'd write a check for £10,000 *cash* and a teller would bring ten packs of neatly rubber-banded thousand-punt notes to a scale, weigh them, and see if they weighed in as £10,000. (They must *know* what £10,000 weighs.) Then the cash would be put in a brown paper bag, which we'd hand over to Johnnie K., who would toss it onto the floor of his van.

Our other job, though it was more of a goal, was to find what is called "painted Irish" furniture. Dog put us in touch with Frank, whose famous emporium is way off the beaten track.

Our directions were: "Locate the large crucifix up on the mountains by Drimoleague. Drive straight to it. Turn up the windy road. And when you see a lot of old rubbish and cars out in the field in front of an apricot-painted farmhouse, there's Frank and his furniture."

Surrounding the house, all higgledy-piggledy, were barnfuls of worn-out wooden furniture. Some were propped up against cow stalls and ricks of hay, some just lay on the ground in various stages of rotted disrepair: dressers painted a hot-pink gloss with a lime-green trim; settle benches in faded ochre and red; wardrobes in magnolia, the ubiquitous cream color found all over Ireland. Out in a field were Victorian bathtubs, sinks and cisterns, ornate gates, copper drainpipes, and broken chimney pots. In another field were six or eight decrepit cars inhabited by dogs and a few itinerant men who "helped" Frank out.

Faced with such bounty—painted treasures we had seen only in books—our task was to separate junk from true dereliction, not an easy job for the untrained eye. But our eyes had begun to be trained by Claudia Kinmouth, who wrote a book called *Painted Irish Furniture*, published by Yale University Press in 1993.

Interest in painted Irish furniture had been modest until recently, for it was considered old-fashioned junk. It was the stuff left in an old house to be put in a pile and burnt. This is no exaggeration. Since I'm on the lookout for it, and ask around, I always get the same response:

"Oh yes, I know it well. The old house was full of it. Didn't we take it all out there to the field a few years ago and burn the lot."

And to the untrained eye, it can look like junk. Some of it is. But this pine furniture, designed by local eighteenth- or nineteenth-century artisans, once furnished every house in Ireland. At its best, it's been preserved by the continued application of glossy paint. At its worst, the furniture is stripped of its glossy paint, denuded of the quirkiness of the nineteenth-century farmer who decided to use apple-green and pink paint to spruce up his furniture for the most important event his house would ever have the honor of hosting—the Stations. That is when Mass was said in the house. And that is when painted furniture was repainted. Since the Stations rotated throughout a parish, the same furniture would be repainted in, say, another four years in totally different colors.

In the nineteenth century, dressers were crammed with unmatched china. A settle was put by the fire and slept upon as an extra bed. Straight-back or large Windsor-style chairs were placed to the side of the fireplace for the man of the house to sit in and smoke his pipe. And in the West Room, a small shelf, called the holy shelf, always supported a picture of the Sacred Heart lit by a red light.

Geoffrey and I love this furniture. Yet its upkeep is not *sans souci*, and many find it garish. To love this furniture and feature it in the way it was intended, it must be painted, and painted, and painted until it's so glossy you can practically see your reflection in it. It must not be stripped back to the pine, which is what happens when it is shipped to America and bought by fancy stores like Bloomingdale's.

Anyway, coming down the hill to meet us is Frank. And Frank's a dresser. He wears a tweed jacket and jodhpurs and carries a mobile phone. He is also a swift talker.

"Oh, yis d'en, Missus, dis is d'real t'ing. Ye won't git dis stuff anywhere at all in Ireland but right here."

He sees me running my hand over the high gloss of a dresser that—considering it's lying in a pile of hay—is in good condition.

"Oh yis, d'en, Missus, y'have d'good eye."

And I do. I even bargain a bit with old Frank for a dresser, a fleet of chairs in cream, lime, baby blue, and red, a wardrobe, a claw-foot bathtub with a drainpipe indicating waste, and a blisteringly heavy jelly cupboard painted gray and sporting decorative crosshatch whittling. Best of all, I find a pair of stone lions ("Lions?" says Geoffrey; "Lions!" say I) that Frank swore had come from the Bishop of Carberry's residence in Rosscarberry.

We're thrilled with our purchases, which Frank promises to keep for us till the house is ready. Our plan is to return in August and move into the stables. Dog's Body swears all will be tickety boo. On the last day of our visit I present Johnnie K. with a ceremonial bottle of Paddy, which he places on the holy shelf, and Geoffrey and I happily return to New York.

ON A WEEKEND BETWEEN RENTERS, we walk through the house and gardens of Magic Flute. We are mourning and meditating on our past, wondering what we'll do with all our stuff when we sell this house.

"Someday Janie's chaise will look fabulous in the Big House."

And yet I know full well that *this* corner—the windowed corner framed by an old cherry tree, one of the few cherry trees to survive the '39 hurricane—will not look the same without the chaise, to whomever buys our house.

"And Stephen's paneling?"

Geoffrey gazes around the room, fitted out with oak paneling more suited for a library. Oak in a beach house? That's the kind of house Magic Flute is. When Stephen died of AIDS, we got his paneling.

"Remember that Thanksgiving . . . how it barely fit into the back of that station wagon. . . ."

"We barely had money to rent it."

"We have to take the paneling with us."

"I know."

The paneling, the chaise, the room, the light, the windows, the cherry tree. What once filled us with joy now fills us with sorrow. A late-spring rain rinses down the flagstone path.

At the bottom of the hill—threaded through with ivy, blue myrtle, and lilies of the valley—lies the cartouche that had been once part of the exterior of Jean Dalrymple's town house. "And the cartouche . . . ?"

Years ago, whenever I was near Park Avenue, I'd walk by Miss D.'s house to try and remember Mammie. To maybe catch a glimpse of her. Anyway, one day I found the house a whisker away from being demolished. It was a shell, gutted, its windows poked out, lathing exposed, roofline smashed in. Yet despite the carnage, the della Robbia–style cartouche of a bowl of blue-and-white flowers remained in place over the front door of this lovely house. This wonderful house. This house I used to think of as *my* house.

It was destined that I save it. I had been guided here this very day to do so. I approached the doorman next door with my telephone number. Please, please, if you see anyone in charge, please. Sure, Miss. I'll call you, Miss, the minute they come with the bulldozers.

But he didn't. Every week I'd go up for a peek. The house was still there. Rained into. Sunned on. Blown asunder. Every surface Mammie ever wiped. Every window I ever shined. All that was beautiful was gone.

Weeks passed, and one day the house was gone, too. Vanished like the village of Brigadoon, soon to be replaced by a high-rise. I stood on the corner of Park and Fifty-fifth Street and gazed across to nothingness. It was all but a handful of dust.

I crossed the street to what was now a vacant lot. I wanted to stand in the rubble. I wanted to invoke the house where I learned about Style, Grace, and Beauty. Never again would I walk down my favorite block in New York—"right off Park," Mammie would say—to try to catch a glimpse of her hurrying down the block, hat on head, gloves on hands.

A gap in the fence allowed me to slip in. And there in the rubble of brick and mortar, propped up in a corner, was my cartouche. It was a blessing. It was a sign. I felt as triumphant as Parsifal finding the Holy Grail.

The cartouche was cracked in two pieces, one big, one little. The demolition crew would have had to crack it to get it out of the wall. There was no way I could lift it myself. I marched over to Park Avenue and hailed a cab, an old Checker, and asked the Israeli driver if he would help. He picked up the big piece as if it were a cookie.

"This is nothing; I have just come back from kibbutz," he said.

We got it down to the Village. But it was Scott and Geoffrey who got it out to Magic Flute.

That was a few years ago. Just enough time for the cartouche to settle into the sand, the swale, the Virginia creeper, and the ivy of Fire Island. It had become a part of the landscape. And yet if anything symbolized my past, running from that sad house in Astoria, to Manhattan, to Mammie's home in Carrigeen—"*Home*, Alice M'rie"—it was Jean Dalrymple's cartouche.

"Don't you think we should leave it here?" Geoffrey said. "It looks like it belongs here, and we'll need a crane to get it out of here."

"No, it must be in Ireland with me."

Nine bean-rows
will i have there

HENRY V DID NOT HAVE as detailed a plan for storming Agincourt as Geoffrey and I had for August.

We buried Scott's ashes in Magic Flute's garden, where he joined his lover, Jack, and a host of others. Bought a couch in an antique shop in Greenwich Village. Had the couch, sheets, towels, china, pots 'n' pans, candlesticks, CDs, tapes, the boom box (I couldn't do all this without *Parsifal*), cookbooks, our clothes, and clothes from the Scott collection shipped to Ireland. We were practically hopping out of our skins with excitement at the prospect of actually cooking, and sleeping, and making love in our house. So excited that we gave the builder an extra week to knot up loose ends.

But the ends were left dangling. During our Memorial Day weekend trip, and then during another short trip in July, Dog's Body had sworn the stables would be ready for us in August. But they weren't. The nineteen days we spent there in August were the hardest nineteen days we've ever spent anywhere.

As Geoffrey and I drove up the laneway to the stables, our hopes were soaring. Our neighbor Audrey Johnston and her kids had tied a bunch of balloons and a welcome home sign on the cow gate. We knew that Ava Astaire McKenzie, Fred's daughter and a friend of a friend of ours in New York, had dropped off a basket of her homegrown spuds, cabbages, tomatoes, artichokes, and mushrooms. Neighbor Sally Johnston had left a dozen of her hen's fresh eggs and a pot of homemade blackberry jam. Basking in the glow of all this bounty, what could go wrong?

Everything.

Geoffrey and I stood in the rubble, looking at the stables, gaping like two gob shites paralyzed by reality. The stables, now our house, looked so different, so tampered with. Standing with our luggage, shopping bags, case of wine, doodads (an apple-green 1930s Twyfford's sink, f'r God's sake), and the balloons, I couldn't help but wonder whether, just possibly, Geoffrey and I were responsible for this mess. We had changed an order, an ethos, that had stood firm for hundreds of years. We were the interlopers. So this mess was our fault. Then I took the chalkboard eraser to my brain and swooshed it clean. We may be interlopers, but this is not our fault. It's the builder's fault, and that of Dog and Dog's Body.

The terrain looked arid. The stables that once sank into green slime were now secured on a hardscrabble rock bed of cement. The tufts of grass and daisies and draping ivy that once dressed the adjacent hedgerow had been ripped out. And rocks, stones, and pebbles were cast asunder. Building debris was scattered about, as were plastic pipes, metal pipes, metal wire, and cable wire. Piles of sand with shovels stuck in them were everywhere. Plastic bins and milk cartons bobbed in the ancient well. Empty paper bags marked *Irish cement* blew in the wind. And the earth, once so green and lush, was gouged by tractor and truck wheels. Where only a few months before the stables had looked Irish, they now looked like they belonged in the Mojave desert.

And what really gnawed at my heart was that the courtyard looked as if it had been tumbled once again.

The interior of the stables wasn't much better. The walls were as gray and unwelcoming as the Slattery bungalow, oh those many years ago. A fine film of concrete, plaster, and sawdust glazed every surface, and it hung like smoke in the air. Little hillocks piled up in the corners of the floor, much like sand did on Fire Island. When we moved, we crunched.

As Geoffrey and I walked back and forth through the stables, an Ira Gershwin lyric drummed in my head: "The British Museum has lost its charm. The British Museum has lost its charm."

We were like zombies. From parlor to bath to mud to bed to courtyard, we'd pass each other in such a state of disbelief, my mouth remained open to the point of drooling. I started to stoop. And I stooped for the nineteen days we spent there.

No trace of the builder. He was on holiday. As were Dog and Dog's Body. They had all deserted us. Ran off with nary a forwarding phone number. And that was just the beginning. We discovered we had neither electricity, water, nor phone.

This was our house. Our dream made manifest. Our problem. Our "holiday home." You feckin' bastards, this is no holiday.

Our Cristo-wrapped couch stood in the middle of the living room—it, too, covered in silt. Packing boxes emblazoned with large green shamrocks were piled high. John Johnston said that when the moving van came, it was so large it couldn't get up the laneway, so he had to run the boxes up to the stables trip by trip on his tractor.

But the AGA, my AGA (Agrippina, I call her), niched in the wall like a statue of the BVM, saved us during this fortnight of nary a mod con.

The AGA is the apotheosis of stoves, or "cookers," as they call them in Ireland. And though ours was the wrong color (green instead of cream) and had a gimpy door, it was the only thing in the house that actually worked. Diamonds may be a girl's best friend, but as sure as there's light in August, the AGA is my friend.

When cronies called from New York, hoping to hear the worst, I told them the best. I talked about my AGA, the highest feather in my "international lifestyle" cap. Yet as with "ruin" or "acre," they hadn't a clue. New Yorkers, with their dinky galley kitchens in their overpriced apartments, barely know the brand name of their range, much less what an AGA is.

It is simplicity itself, this cooker that was invented and patented by Dr. Gustaf Dalen, the Swedish physicist and Nobel Prize winner. The AGA has no dials to fiddle with. It runs on oil (or solid fuel) and has no pilot light, only a round cylinder emitting a rosy glow. On top, instead of burners, the AGA has two shiny, pizza-large, metal discs. One, called the boiling plate, boils water in a matter of seconds. The other, called the simmer plate, melts butter, sweats onions, and scrambles eggs. Underneath are two ovens operating on radiant heat. One roasts and broils. The other cooks slowly—it makes lovely stews and a killer chili! The AGA also heats the hot-water tank and stays on 365 days a year to ward off damp. It's as beautiful a machine as a Mercedes-Benz. They say Dustin Hoffman owns one, and so does Julia Roberts.

With the AGA and our battery-run boom box, and buckets of water from the well, Geoffrey and I may not have had electricity, but we had music and food. And the weather *was* on our side. That first night was so summery, you'd think we'd have said: Shite! Let's go out and eat! But with the sun not setting till ten and with the prospect of finally cooking in an AGA, I was determined to cook our first meal. Before I could salt a chop, though, we partook in Round I of the nineteen-day ritual of Wiping and Vacuuming. (That first night it took five hours.)

A tick before midnight, the couch was unwrapped, pillows fluffed, candles lit, wildflowers picked, and wine poured. I forged ahead with the ceremonial pork chop and applesauce, which we were too tired to enjoy but hungry enough to eat.

We were dead on our feet and had no bed to sleep in. Mattress, yes. Bed frame, no. We had decided to use a metal Victorian bed frame left in the Big House, and that was rusty. Dog's Body had promised to get the frame sandblasted in Cork but hadn't. So we laid a sheet of plastic on the floor, put the mattress, still encased in its plastic, atop that, and new sheets atop that. To the sounds of cows munching grass right outside the window and neighboring farm dogs barking alarums to one another, we tried to sleep.

The next morning, and every morning thereafter, we were covered in silt. Our eyes were ganky. Our hair was filthy. Weeks later when Dog's Body paid a call and we told him about the silt, he said, "Oh yes, d'house is settling."

When the Electrical Supply Board (ESB) ultimately came to turn on the electricity, which in turn turned on the pump that turned on the water, we had a laugh. Johnnie K. told us how our well was dug. A local water diviner arrived with a divining rod that quivered like a willow in a windstorm when it found the watery place where the well would be drilled. Of course, this being the twentieth century, we would be using electricity to draw the water from the well to the house, not an old-fashioned pump.

Anyway, when we finally had running water, we had no place to shower. But that was our fault, our fault entirely. Our glorious six-foot-long claw-footed Victorian bathtub had a bath tray arrayed with every bubble bath and perfumed oil known to Lady Macbeth. But at the suggestion of installing a shower, we had cried, No, no! If ever there were eschewers of modernity, happy to grovel at the shrine of authenticity (imagining long, luxuriating, *Women in Love*–by-the-firelight baths), we were they. We hadn't factored in that silt and dust are best showered off, not sat in.

There was no lovemaking that night, nor any other of the eighteen remaining nights. Fie on my Wagnerian visions of Tristan and Isolde—Isolde, who was Irish, f'r God's sake, dying in ecstasy in gritty landscapes. With a few draughts of mead we might have tried to make love, but dust and dirt defeated our ardor in August.

With neither a land phone nor a mobile phone, we drove to Bantry several times a day and hit the booths to call the ESB, the plumber, and Telecom Eireann. Oh yes, oh yes, we'll send someone out straightaway. But they didn't. They wouldn't. And we knew it. Months ago, Johnnie K. had silenced Geoffrey, who was acting like a little wet hen. Quivering with New York anxiety about how slowly the work was going, Geoffrey said, "We won't have enough time."

Johnnie K. replied, "When God made time, he made plenty of it." We thought this quaint then, but now we knew it was accurate. This is Ireland, the land where time means nothing.

We'd call the architect, get the answering machine, and scream, "We need help! Where are you?! We don't know what to do! Have you deserted us?" He didn't respond either.

Mop in hand (for believe you me, slate floors hold on to dirt), I'd say things like "We gotta get this show on the road." Then Geoffrey would say, "When is stupidity bravery and bravery stupidity?" Arid I'd say, "It's a long way to Tipperary." Then we'd get into the car, put on Frank Sinatra, and go take a shower in the "leisure center" of a local hotel whose pool and Jacuzzi were always filled with women and children. On the way to town we'd stop at the Johnstons' to see if we had any mail.

John and Audrey Johnston and their five children live in a modern house. They serve as silent reminders that I am a woman alone, an only child, a motherless child, a woman without children. Not that they do anything to provoke these thoughts. They simply live their lives as their parents did before them. It's Geoffrey and I who choose to lead our lives differently. As Sally Johnston, John's mother, remarked when we told her we'd decided not to have children: "Ye've no one to please but yer selves."

Geoffrey and I stand out here, and not just because we wear black. In a community united by faith, family, and farmland, we must seem strange, childless couple that we are, fixing up a ruin. For whom? We don't even have heirs to leave the house to. We only have each other.

It's a rare occurrence when I don't walk back over the fields after visiting the Johnstons and not think thoughts of home.

Home, Alice M'rie.

I look at Audrey and her brood of chicks and I'm filled with a mixture of puzzlement and loss. I've lost touch with what it's like to have a mother. If Mammie were alive, she'd be ninety-one years old. I don't know, would I still call her Mammie? And I don't know, would she still call me Alice M'rie? I do know I've not turned out the way she wanted. And since I've forgotten the sound of her voice (other than "*Home*, Alice M'rie"), I invent an Irish patois that scolds more than it praises: "Alice M'rie, ye've dyed yer hair and ye're not a teacher. Ye lived with a man, for how many years before marrying him? Ye ran from home, moved to Greenwich Village, and ye now live in a ruin in Ireland. A ruin! What can I tell them at home? I ran from Ireland to better myself in New York. And now ye wind up back in County Cork no less. Not even Kerry. Living in a ruin."

If self-pity grabs the hasp of my arse, I hear Carey happily crowing: "Ye're a failure an' th' devil's stuck in th' seat of yer pants. That's why ye've gone back. Like th' song says, ye couldn't *make* it in New York."

The contrast couldn't be greater between the way the Johnston kids are growing up and the way I did. They live in the now and the new. Neither mired in the past nor ruled by the Catholic Church, the Johnstons, like many of my neighbors, are Protestant. They are nice, normal, churchgoing Irish citizens. So normal, I sometimes think I've wandered into another world when I come down for the mail.

"Hello, hello, Alice, don't bother with that now," Audrey says as I stomp the muck off my boots. "You see how we are here."

See! I see everything sparkling.

The Johnstons use "you," not "ye."

Kids are all over the place. Flashes of myself, always with a book and always quiet, pop into my head. Since everything I know about children comes from the *New York Times*, I figure the kids are "acting out." Then I realize they're just being kids, something I know nothing about.

In the corner, *Titanic* plays on a mute TV. Broadway actor Victor Garber is gazing at a clock sliding down a mantel. His ship is going down and he will go down with it. Relief floods over me. Here's something I can relate to.

"That's Victor Garber. He sings in musical shows in New York." Silence. That I know Garber sings is of no interest. Now if I knew Baby Spice . . .

John Johnston comes in from the cows, leaving his muddy boots in the vestibule. The two littlest children, Yvonne and John Jr., start chanting, "Daddy,

Daddy . . ." beseeching their father to slice a cupcake in half for them. Taking out a pocketknife, Johnston cradles a pink-iced cupcake in his large hand, splits it in two, gives the iced half to one child and the cake half to the other. I think of Carey, who was raised to be a farmer but fled instead to America to become (possibly) "the playboy of the Western world" and wound up a janitor in the Roxy Theater.

Cupcake gulped, the kids' never-ending procession to the fridge resumes. They open it. Close it. Open it. Close it. They're on the prowl for juice, cheese, chips, yogurt, biscuits, chocolate. I sit there gob smacked. Our ice box in Astoria never held such bounty. Why are these children consuming empty calories? And *sweets*! Yet I know my motherless standards do not apply here. (I have never eaten between meals in my life.) The Johnston kids are modern kids raised by parents who are blissfully at ease with themselves. At least they all sit together in the one room glancing at *Titanic*, and not snarling, sad, and silent, in separate rooms like Carey, Mammie, and me.

Bored with the slowness of the sinking ship, the two oldest girls, Elaine and Rachel, walk back up to the house with me. Entering the stables, they notice a pair of bluebird prints lying on a box. Elaine gives them the eye. "Where will you put them?"

I tell them they were my mammie's. She had told me she bought them in the five-and-ten when she was pregnant with me. For her to reveal even this little scrap of information was unusual, for Mammie never mentioned the past.

The bluebirds are part of what I've left of her stuff, along with a silver letter opener, a sewing basket, a silver thimble stamped *Killarney*, three Best & Co. hats, a rhinestone pin, and a yellow linen dress.

The bluebirds hung over Carey and Mammie's twin beds. Besides a small picture of the Blessed Virgin that Mollie (*O poor Mollie*) brought from Lourdes, they were the only adornment in the room. "Framed at Macy's," Mammie would say of the plump little birds tweeting on a branch bursting with apple blossoms.

I watch the girls dance down the lane to their home and their mammie. And I feel a sense of loss. The bluebirds bring me back to Astoria and how, after Mammie was killed, Carey threw all her stuff out.

I knew there was no point confronting him. He was dying for any excuse to clap me across the face. Out went her clothes. Her pocketbooks. The few Christmas ornaments. Even the potato baker, blackened beyond use but still able to produce a tasty potato. He left a few bags of letters and photos. Going through them would take more time than he was willing to give.

The photos are black-and-whites. Snaps, as they called them. They were taken when my parents looked happy, probably way before the War and shortly after they emigrated from Ireland. It's a summer afternoon in the country and Alice and Denis are in a field. A grand house looms in the background, where Alice Slattery may have worked as a maid. She's wearing a striped sunsuit. My father's in chinos.

There they are lying in a hammock.

There they are frolicking with the cows.

There they are wading in a stream.

There they are riding a tractor.

They're in love.

This was long ago. Long before Denis became "Carey" and Mammie became "Big Alice." This was long before Astoria. Long before me. I see Mammie frozen in black-and-white moments of happiness, and I don't know her. I look away in embarrassment. She never spoke about this.

I search out a few snaps with me in them. We're in Astoria. Mammie and I are in the rumble seat of a car. Mammie's looking at Carey, who's taking the picture. She looks sad. They switch places. Carey's next to me. He looks like a wavy-haired blow-ho. These are the people I remember, with their hardened eyes of broken dreams. These are the people I lived with, in that freezing apartment in Astoria.

We're tenants there, not owners. And it cuts Mammie to the quick. Renting a cold-water flat on the top floor of a row house means failure. Carey's, for not being a better provider. And her own, for having a soft heart and marrying him. Paying rent to a landlord, who they say is a firebug, salts her wound and makes her question Carey's sanity.

And yet the house is pretty. There are two large elm trees in front, and out back a magnificent cherry. Across the street are vacant lots overshadowed by the Con Edison gas tanks. A few blocks away flows the East River, although it's hardly pretty. By the time it curves from Manhattan and starts flowing under Hellgate Bridge, its banks grow rocky and rat-infested.

"We're just across the river from Manhattan," coos Mammie in her letters home to Ireland, as if that makes a difference.

On the other side of the house, surrounded by a three-block area of elm, oak, chestnut, and hazel trees, is a Victorian mansion. It's an insane asylum called River Crest, which is as scary as it's inviting. We can hear the patients screaming at night, even with the windows closed.

We've neither heat nor hot water, so we roast in summer and freeze in winter. With no kitchen ventilation, all windows are open to accommodate the rising grease from the never-ending fries. Having to boil water to wash herself isn't the life Mammie envisioned oh so long ago in Ireland, when she ran away from home to marry Denis Carey in a village that even today is but a wide spot on the road.

Night after night, hat on her head to add a touch of class, my mammie stands at the stove, boiling water to wash grease off plates. Carey doesn't seem to mind. Mammie says he came from somewhere remote up in the mountains.

"Old mountaineer," she jibes.

Yet to Carey, Astoria must have been better than living so far up a mountain you get nosebleeds.

Friday night. Radio station WJZ is playing. Carey is snoring away on the couch. Mammie is pressing the pleats of my uniform skirt, and I'm cutting up Mitzi's beef liver and frying it in butter. We're listening to the song John Wayne sipped his pint to in the film *The Quiet Man*.

I've met some folks who say that I'm a dreamer.
And I've no doubt there's truth in what they say.

Forty years later I hear this same song a lot in Bantry. It booms out to the street from O'Brien's Electric Shop, melting into the haze of turf smoke that signals the coming of evening. I stroll around looking at women come and go from Super Valu, their shopping carts full of jumbo-size everything. I never buy jumbo anything.

The song makes me twitchy. O'Brien probably thinks it brings in business. I walk out on the square to have a look at the bay. Nothing worse than Irish-American sentimentality. Yet that song *meant* something to Carey and Mammie, the two of them in that kitchen with all the grease, thinking thoughts of Home.

Home, Alice M'rie.

Down on the quay, the Whiddy Island ferry is pulling out. It's a small one, not like the large Fire Island ferries whizzing back and forth on the Great South Bay on a Friday night, like tonight. On the ferry, people knew me. Sometimes the bonhomie drove me crazy, but now I miss it.

The moon is coming up over the Kerry mountains. Over there beyond Caha, beyond Mangerton, beyond the Healy Pass is . . .

Home, Alice M'rie.

This same moon will shine on ferries going to Fire Island tonight. Shite! O'Brien's put the song on again. And he's bumped up the sound.

But when the moonlight creeps across the rooftops
Of this great city, wondrous though it be
And though they say the streets are paved with
gold dust,
I long to be back home in Innisfree.

A hive for the honey-bee

IT'S FIVE IN THE MORNING and I'm lying on the floor of the stables, quite awake. Little zephyrs of silt light upon me every time I change position, so I don't. It's so still I can faintly hear trans-Atlantic planes as they swing over Cork, making their journey up the Shannon estuary, on to the airport. On one of these planes is our first guest, David La Greca.

David is coming here for our first dinner party—the Gala, as I call it. Invitations—Tiffany's, mind—were mailed from New York a month earlier. Geoffrey and I have been in the stables five days now, without electricity or phone, although yesterday the electrician popped by for a sec. ("I'm on my way to Hare Island," he said, happy as a clam. Irish electricians always seem to be going to Hare Island.) He got one socket going and the water pump working, so we can bathe without going to the leisure center (oh, t'ank God). Feck electricity, I say. Agrippina and I will triumph.

David is the first close friend I made after Scott and everyone preceding him died of AIDS. I met him on the Long Island Rail Road coming back from Fire Island, where I appeared in a production of the musical

Damn Yankees. David introduced himself, saying he'd seen the show.

"You played that sports reporter like she was Diana Vreeland."

We chat. The train comes. I say I don't talk with people on the train because I write. He says he writes, too. And, of course, we never shut up. I took him to the first preview of Stephen Sondheim's *Passion*, which was so unbearable that he reached over, touched my knee, and said, "This is worse than the Stations of the Cross." That cemented our friendship. That David is gay and an AIDS activist endeared him to my heart. But what touched me most was that he was once a priest. A few years later David La Greca invited himself to Ireland.

We found him standing at the apex of the village, framed by a nineteenth-century coaching house, all togged out in his new lemon-yellow, I'll-face-the-rain-of-Ireland jacket. He was going in and out of the shops, wondering if anyone knew how to get to our house.

I let out the Fire-Island-Whoop-of-Recognition first, then David did, then Geoffrey. Hallelujah! Jesus! La Greca would bear witness to our chaos. Our shite. He'd brought us Sunday's *New York Times* and *Dubliners.*

"Listen, doll, I know you have a copy in New York, but you need one for Ireland."

He didn't bring a traveling crucifix in its own little box to stand next to his bed, the way Father Bob did. Not that he had a bed to sleep in. La Greca had the couch.

Back in New York, he'd oohed and aahed over pictures of our place, but nothing had prepared him for how dirty everything was. Threading through the rubble, cup of tea in hand, he noted, "Well, guys, it is stone. Do you know what they'd pay for these rocks on Fire Island?"

Once his inspection was over, La Greca spun into action. Having been in the priesthood stood him in good stead. He hooked up our washing machine. "Just like being in the seminary in Belgium."

Then he took the fleet of painted chairs and washed them down outside. "Just like being back in the Missions."

Then he looked at paint chips. "Dad was in the paint business."

I'm in the house, washing down the floor again and I see La Greca, wearing a red Lacoste polo shirt, outside washing windows. I feel more than a little odd. The last time I was in an Irish house with a priest was in Carrigeen with Father Bob. Father Bob, always wearing his Roman collar except for when he wore his dressing gown. I hope nothing bad will happen to me here. I go out to the rocks for a few deep breaths. Yet Father Bob, a lit Sweet Afton dangling from the side of his mouth, comes along with me.

Father Bob and I would ride around Killarney in his black Morris Minor, looking at the sights. The Paps of Anu come into view. Two pyramidal mountaintops, capped with Bronze Age funeral cairns, giving the appearance of two Botticelli-shaped female breasts with nipples, belonging to the mother of the gods.

"Here we are, then, Alice M'rie, under the Paps. Sure you don't want a drag?"

I take a few more deep breaths. Priests . . . I'm still afraid of them. My musing is broken by Elaine and Rachel, who bring up eggs and a big bunch of wild-flowers. They stare at the three of us trying to put order in a house where order never existed. The girls know the stables as the place their father housed sick calves. As for La Greca—it's hard enough for them to get used to Geoffrey and me, but a guy wearing shorts, polo shirt, and a cap, who says, "I've seen pictures of you two girls," well, it was clearly a little unsettling.

IT IS THE NIGHT OF THE GALA. If Brueghel were an Irish painter, he would have captured this hay-golden August day as it flowed into night. Who needs electricity with the sun still golden at ten? Candlelight and the glow from oil lamps caress the unpainted stone walls.

An oversized linen tablecloth covering a few planks creates snowy mounds on the floor. Lovely Agrippina is cooking a stuffed pork roast on one oven rack while Ava's potatoes, simmering with cream and pancetta, are on the other one. A frying pan filled with Bramley apples and South African lemons bubbles away on the simmering plate. And some chilled white wine? Well, my dear, it's been cooling in the well.

Musicals blast out to the fields. Only happy ones. *Guys and Dolls* melts into *La Cage Aux Folles* and merges with *Kiss Me Kate* to blend into *Cabaret* and become *A Little Night Music*.

> *A weekend in the county*
> *So exhausting that you have to lie down.*

La Greca puts on his blazer, Geoffrey and I our all-purpose black, and we wait for the first human guests these stables have ever witnessed. The humming music from *Butterfly* would be appropriate now, for the crickets are chirping an August rift. Amidst the rubble, looking over the mountains toward Bantry Bay, we stand, three New Yorkers bound by the friendship of another island and by the scars of a terrible disease. Comfortable silence, holy silence, descends on us.

"It's like a benediction," says La Greca.

And he smiles.

Down the way, cars whir by on the road on their way to Schull, Skibbereen, Ballydehob, Ahakista, Castletownbere, Glengarriff, or Kilcrohane. Over the Goat's Path. Up from the Sheep's Head. Down from the Mizen. Romantic names all. Three cars are heading to us.

Geoffrey and I have made friends here through the magic circle of "six degrees of separation." Take Ava

Astaire McKenzie. She and her husband, portrait painter Richard McKenzie, have lived in West Cork for more than twenty-five years. At Gay Men's Health Crisis, Geoffrey worked with Lars Jahns, who once worked for the American Film Institute in Hollywood. When Lars heard we were thinking of buying a house in Cork, he told us to call Ava. Now she and Richard are our courage here, Richard having sealed our fate by saying, "Yes, there is an aura about West Cork."

Ava and Richard in turn told us to call drama critic and Yale professor Gordon Rogoff and his partner, artist Morton Lichter, who happen to actually live nearby. On that Thanksgiving when we first saw this house, we gave them a call. Our fate was sealed once more over mince tarts and wine.

Gordon and Morton then introduced us to the Collins sisters, Moira and Deirdre, standard-bearers of West Cork mores and good taste. If this sounds like a Philip Barry comedy with so-and-so knowing so-and-so, who is married to the ex-wife of so-and-so, it's true. West Cork is that way. Geoffrey and I may be planning to leave Fire Island, but we have found another spot, on another island, where everyone knows everyone else's business.

The three cars arrive at once. People start to squeal as they hobble over the rubble.

"You two . . . you two . . ."

"You are sooooooo smart to let the Big House go for a while."

"Be careful, marriages break up redoing old houses."

Although everyone has seen the progress that was made on the stables during the past few months, seeing our ruin by candlelight is magic. People troop from room to room and back again, admiring the fuchsia August sunset that catches tussle mussies of daisies, montbretia, loosestrife, and Queen Anne's lace placed on every windowsill. In the deep purple of it all, even the gray cement walls take on a medieval glow.

I launch into how much I love the custom of painting the outside of old Irish houses in vivid colors. It's what I want to ultimately do with the Big House. But Deirdre says that Jeremy Irons, who lives in a restored old house just east of here, loves his gray cement walls and is letting them be.

Soon everyone is sitting around on the painted chairs, drinking wine and callooing and callaying. Richard McKenzie keeps walking back and forth with me, muttering, "Remarkable, remarkable . . . I remember, I remember. . . ."

In this stable that has never heard a note of music, we play tunes by famous 1930s dance bands and songs by Cole Porter, Noël Coward, Rodgers and Hart. Dreamy stuff for an intoxicating night.

I look out the Dutch door to a full August moon and think, My God, this is it. Feck electricity and phone. All one needs is water, the oil-fueled AGA, candles, and a battery-powered boom box.

Dizzy with exhaustion and wine and triumph, for we did pull it off, I start quoting Auntie Mame: "Oh, no more champagne, Lord Dudley. The bubbles no longer tickle my nose." And I say it over and over again.

Ava takes pictures and people dance—Moira and La Greca outside on the rubble, Geoffrey and me in front of the AGA. We feel like Romans shimmying in the temple of Hera.

As Geoffrey and I dance, I'm seeing us when we were young. When we were actors, foolish and living on unemployment. How we lived together for twenty years without ever feeling the need to marry. Marriage was for other people, for people whose relationships needed help, or whose parents insisted. Then bad things started to happen. I almost died from a new and baffling disease called eosinophilia-myalgia syndrome. Geoffrey's parents both died unexpectedly. And AIDS started to kill all our close friends.

In 1991, Jack Hefton had just died, and Scott was none too well. We were out in the Grove, in the kitchen making dinner, and Scott said, "Listen, guys, how many more memorials can we take? Why don't you two get married and give us something to celebrate." Easy for him to say. Mammie would not have been pleased with my talking about anything to do with marriage, even with her penchant for going to weddings back there in Astoria.

Miss D.'s crony, the actress Rita Gam, was to blame. She was palsy-walsy with Grace Kelly and was going to Monaco for the wedding. If Rita hadn't been so fluffed up at the prospect of being Grace's bridesmaid, Mammie wouldn't have gotten so fluffed up about weddings.

Rita's helping herself to another cup of tea.

"Why, Big Alice, you're such a help to Jean, I'd love if you'd come to Monaco with me and help out."

Nothing more's made of it. We don't go. Thee-aticals (as Carey would say) say things like that over cups of tea. Instead, Mammie and I start catching weddings.

"Come on, Alice M'rie," she'd say, "let's catch a wedding."

It's a Friday night in June. Carey's sitting at the kitchen table, slurping his tea and reading the *Long Island Star* obits under his breath. Mammie's standing at the stove cooking up well-done chops on a high flame. She's flushed from the run to Horn & Hardart for Carey's rice pudding and the fruit cocktail to drown it in. Fat's spattering all over the place, so Mammie's turned the veil over the brim of her hat, leaving her face free to absorb the steam and grease.

Suddenly Carey sniffs and sucks the tea leaves through his teeth. He's hit on a good one.

"Well, old Moynihan's finally keeled over. Bet he didn't have a nickel to leave the wife."

Mammie gives me the side eye. "She was probably dying to get rid of him." The conversation ends. It's come to the point where Alice and Denis speak only about who died, how they died, and if they left any money.

"Er, Al . . . pour us some grease over them chops."

She does. I go to the sink and wash grease off my plate. Miss D. doesn't allow grease in her kitchen. I look at the clock; it's six-thirty. We've sixteen hours to go before we can catch a wedding.

Every Saturday morning, with but a scant cup of tea in our bellies, Mammie and I flee the house and make a beeline for the Mac. Arm in arm like school chums, we weave our way through block after block of pretty houses with front gardens all abloom with June red roses.

"Alice M'rie, stop calling the Immaculate Conception the Mac."

"That's what all the kids call it."

"And stop saying kids. A kid is a goat. Sisters used to teaching children like the Kennedys haven't come all the way out here on the subway to teach goats in a school called the Mac. It's the Immaculate Conception. Say that now."

Mammie's impressed, as we all are, that the Sisters of the Sacred Heart of Jesus and Mary also teach the Kennedys.

We chat. Never about Carey, or grease, or Ireland, or anything pertaining to ourselves. What we crave is firsthand gossip from Dorothy Kilgallen. Or better still, a hot flash from Miss D.

"Do ye know who was on the phone yesterday? . . ."

Rosemary Clooney, of all people! And do ye know what Homer told me? He said when Joe was up the street there in City Center, in that play of Miss D.'s—

101

Mammie calls José Ferrer Joe!

"—he'd have the poor girl round to his dressing room at intermission." Having Rosemary "round" sounds a little spicy.

With a word, Mammie's begun to weave her magic spell about Sex, Marriage, and Men.

José Ferrer, with an accent mark. Homer says it's Ho-Say. Not Josie. Ho-Say. Sounds a little common to me. Now, Andre. Andre. Without an accent. Andre Porimbeanu, the chauffeur who ran off with the rich girl, Gamble Benedict. Gamble, named for the vice. Who can she pray to? Andre . . . Andre Porimbeanu. I must learn to say it correctly in case I run into him on Park Avenue, whilst walking Chindu, Miss D.'s little dog. Pooooooh. Rhummmmm. Bay-an-euuuuuuu. Oh, how beautifully it glides off my lips. That's a name with real glamour, style, class, and money. It's not the Irish who've the money. It's the foreigners.

Nearly ten. With a frighteningly accurate internal clock, Mammie grabs my hand and quickens her pace.

"Come on, Alice M'rie, let's catch a wedding."

We figure out the lavishness of the wedding by the number of cars parked in front of the church. If the girl's family is of slender means, there might be just the one rented Caddy for herself and her father. Sometimes the means are even slenderer and there are no rented cars at all. Just borrowed. Frugality like this doesn't interest us. Mammie and I fatten on splendor.

Oh, but our spirits rise as we round Deutsch Brothers' corner and see a whole fleet of gleaming black Caddies parked outside the church. Dave comes out, wipes his hands on his bloody apron, and bows low to Mammie.

"Top of the morning to you, Mrs. Denis." Mind, he never calls her Mrs. Carey. Maybe he thinks she's Auntie Mame.

"Dave, I want a roast beef. Save the first cut for me."

The little extra money from Miss D. lets Mammie indulge her interest in fancy cuts of meat.

From our vantage point at Deutsch's, we assess the event. Depending on the crowd, we stay in front of the shop, or move across the street to mingle with the guests. Mammie and I always dress like guests. That's our assimilation trick. We always look invited. Always perfectly coordinated. She in beige and black, me in plaid or navy.

In stony anticipation, we wait for the bride to alight from the car. Excitement mounts. Our hearts beat the faster. This is the big moment. This will determine the rest of our day. In the few seconds it takes the bride to enter the church with her father (who doesn't hold a tick of interest for us), Mammie and I make a decision about whether to stay or go. This decision rests solely on the wedding dress. If the dress looks worthy of our attention, we slip into the church at the top of the Mass and sit in the back on the bride's side.

Mammie claims she can spot a good dress by the hemming. A good wedding dress, from a store like Lord &

Taylor, has a substantial hem that adds weight, so the skirt can swing gracefully. A dress from a ho-hum store like Gimbel's hasn't much of a hem at all, just a turn up and stitching. But woe to the bride who wears a wedding dress so purposefully plain or ostentatiously fancy that it whispers "homemade." A dress like that is too sad to discuss, and we immediately leave.

In our rating of wedding dresses, "okay" or "pretty" do not the mustard cut. Mammie and I crave the alpha or the omega, the divine or the atrocious. We settle for nothing less. It's the end of the fifties, and theme weddings are stylish, so our wish is granted more often than not. If enduring a long, dreary Mass insures us days and days of couturier discussion, we stay for another look at the dresses and a glimpse of the groom as the couple walks down the aisle in married bliss.

Decorum is all. Off-the-cuff comments or little gasps of horror are discouraged, no matter how big a travesty it is.

Our omega: O Horror Sublime—the Indian Summer Wedding. The day coincides with Halloween. Eight bridesmaids and two flower girls, clad in a descending chromatic array of orange, gold, and yellow. Little sequined pumpkins stitched into the ribbons of the bridesmaids' bouquets of cascading autumnal leaves, surrounding an overstuffed bunch of nasty mums. This is our glorious omega. Princess Grace was a fool not to do the same.

Our alpha: The Snowball Wedding. Gerry's a rich girl. Her father's a doctor and she's marrying one, an older one with gray hair and a mustache. Mammie has it in for mustaches. Here all the girls wear white and carry oversized bouquets of white hydrangea called Snowballs. The girls are very pretty. They look like the Twelve Dancing Princesses. The bride's long hair is pulled into a chignon like Princess Grace. Sprays of hydrangea and baby's breath are tucked around her massive head of gold, giving the effect of a halo. It's so elegant, swelligant, I forget we're in Astoria.

Three months later the couple separates. An annulment is granted. Mammie doesn't explain what annulment is. Oh, but it's bad. It's really bad. I hear the way the old hens cluck on the A&P checkout line.

"What happened to that *poor* girl?!"

It must've been something to do with having a girl round. Mammie and I drop the Snowball Wedding from our chats.

After poor Gerry's extravaganza, little hints of foreboding sneak into our chats. We'd be standing in front of Deutsch Brothers, waiting to catch a wedding, when suddenly Mammie would sniff and say, "Well, Alice M'rie, I'd rather be an old man's dolly than a young man's slave."

"Mammie, is that Shakespeare?"

Mammie says nothing. But every time she'd get an opening, like looking at wedding pictures in the *Long*

Island Star, she'd repeat it: "I'd rather be an old man's dolly than a young man's slave."

Without weddings to break the monotony, my days are always the same. School, then Miss D.'s. If we didn't start getting these letters from Ireland, badgering Mammie to bring "the girl"—that's what they call me—"Home," we wouldn't have much to chat about.

Mammie opens a Christmas Club to save up for the trip Home. She starts saying, "We're going Home, Alice M'rie . . . *Home*." And she says it all the time. But we can't afford to save more than a dollar or two a week. Mammie never asks Miss D. for a raise. She's like Carey that way, believing that if she asks for something, she'll get a no.

Then something happens. One Saturday as we're leaving the Mac after catching a wedding, Mammie says, "We're going into the city to help out Jed Harris. Miss D. says he needs us on Saturdays."

Jed Harris would freeze the poetry in your soul. Many's the time I'd see his greatcoated figure as he strode up the stairs for his rendezvous with Miss D. If I ran into him, I'd give him a wide berth. *Wide*, I tell you. Jed Harris looks dark. Evil. He has the hooded eyes of the serpent in the Garden of Eden. Cloaked in cigarette smoke, his greatcoat fills the width of the stairs.

Jed is Tweedledum to the Tweedledee of Henry Luce. Mammie says they're Miss D.'s gentleman callers. One comes calling on Tuesday, the other on Thursday. To signify his presence, Jed leaves his fedora and camel hair coat on the chair in the hall. Henry leaves his cane. We've no idea what goes on up there, but when the men go upstairs, we stay downstairs.

Henry Luce is *Life* magazine, but I don't give a fig about him. It's his wife I care about. Clare Boothe Luce is Catholic and the U.S. representative to the Vatican. She's holy, too. She's always in the Sunday supplements, clad in a black mantilla and clutching a pair of crystal rosary beads. Mammie's so impressed with Miss Clare's nearness to the Pope, she thinks Henry's weekly visit to Miss D. will bring a little bit of papal grandeur to Fifty-fifth Street.

Anyway, there we are waiting for the Madison Avenue bus. "There's lots of bakeries up there by Jed," says Mammie.

Bakery. Bribery.

What a beautiful word, *bakery*. Bakeries filled with jelly cookies dusted with powdered sugar. Bakeries crammed with orange cupcakes filled with cream. Blackout cakes. Othellos. Jelly-roll blues.

"Is he near Babka?" I ask, knowing Madison Avenue like the back of my hand. "There's a Babka at Seventy-second."

"Jed's just around the corner," says Mammie.

The bus stops right at Babka. Maybe I'll get a cookie there for tea. Mammie and I get off and proceed to Jed's sublet on Seventy-third Street.

Broadway producer and director Jed Harris was born Jacob Horowitz in 1900 in Newark, New Jersey. He claimed he was the first Jew ever admitted to Yale. Everyone said he was a genius. And he acted like one. At age twenty-eight, he produced four smash hits on Broadway in the space of eighteen months, a feat never again matched. In his heyday, Jed Harris was one of the most feared and hated men in show business.

Mammie says Dorothy Kilgallen says Jed is in New York working on Ernie Kovacs's movie *Operation Mad Ball*. He is also producing two Broadway plays and writing a *Twilight Zone* episode with Rod Serling. However, if the truth be known, Jed is down on his luck, possibly even washed up.

This is what Homer tells us about Jed: Jed Harris is such a son of a bitch that Laurence Olivier (after being directed by him in *The Green Bay Tree*) modeled his screen portrayal of *Richard III* on him, right down to the "Jewish" nose, patent-leather hair, and hunch. Walt Disney modeled the Big Bad Wolf after him. And Noël Coward said Jed reminded him of a praying mantis.

"Homer, who's Noël Coward?"

"Dwa-ling, he is the Master."

Mammie loves that we're going to work for Jed Harris. The Jed Harris who directed *Our Town*. The Jed Harris who has a "love child" with actress Ruth Gordon. The Jed Harris who has the good taste to be in love with the same person Mammie's in love with—Jean Dalrymple.

Jed's expecting us. Mammie says Miss D. said he wouldn't mind me around, for I'm quiet. I read. I help out. Oh, I'm a great help. We ring the bell. No answer. We ring again. Jed bellows, "It's open." We go into a darkened, smoky, dusty, mustard-colored, smelly, whiskey'ed apartment.

"Is that Big Alice and *the* Little Miss Alice?" His voice sounds as if we just woke him up. Yet it's already noon. "Come back here this instant."

We march into Jed Harris's bedroom, a room in which before long I would look forward to spending the greater part of my Saturdays.

Mammie and I always have the same routine. We get there by noon. Jed's apartment is dark and he's always in bed. He stays there all day pretending to sleep, hoping the phone will ring. We change into our uniforms in a windowless room known as "the maid's room." Jed doesn't care one way or the other what we wear, but Mammie likes the uniforms—blue in winter, yellow in summer. My long hair's hoisted into a severe bun so it won't fall in my face.

"Alice M'rie, no one wants to see a hair, other than their own, on the bed linen."

I look like a little witch.

Key in the door. *Bang!* goes the kettle.

"Jed, do ye want tea?"

"I want Earl Grey's 'Twine.' None of your peasant brew." And Jed and I laugh. I'm sitting at the bottom of his bed. He's propped up with a million pillows. There's not a hair on them. Jed's pretty bald.

"Little Alice, how is your cat? I trust you've given her a suitable name?"

"Mitzi, after Mitzi Gaynor . . ."

"The most talentless woman ever to blight the screen. She turns the silver screen to tin."

"Awww, Jed, she's cute. Didn't you see her in *There's No Business Like Show Business?*" Ignoring my love of common spectacle, Jed bellows for Mammie. "Alice . . . the tea. I'm trying to educate your daughter about who's good in the pictures and who's pig swill."

Mammie arrives with a tea tray, which she places on the bed between us. "Jed, Alice M'rie doesn't use language like that."

"Big Alice, have a cup with us." Jed Harris straightens himself up in the bed.

Oh, Jed Harris's bed. I see his hairy chest, and hairy upper arms, and hairy back. Terrible. Yet he has a love child, not just a child, but a *love* child. I don't know what it means. But it sounds spicy. Oh, who's afraid of the big bad wolf, the big bad wolf, the big bad wolf? I am. I am . . . a little.

"Jed, there's too much to do. Alice M'rie must start cleaning her ashtrays."

Jed winks at me and lights up a Salem.

The small bedroom is always dark. It holds only one piece of furniture, the bed. Its headboard, a bookcase, is crammed to overflowing with every book in the world. They spill on the floor and onto the bed.

Scattered about is every newspaper printed. The *London Times*. The *Wall Street Journal*. The *Washington Post*. The *Los Angeles Times*. *Paris Match*, the *Tatler*, and the *Economist*. Trickling through the bed linen are piles of loose change. *Piles*, I tell you. Oh, the silver quarters! Mine as a reward when I answer a Harris question correctly.

"Little Alice, from whose house does the light from yonder window break?"

"Awww, Jed, that's easy. It's Juliet's."

"And . . . and . . . and?"

"It is the East . . . and . . ." I get so embarrassed.

"Yes?"

"And Juliet is the sun."

"Brava!"

Jed Harris proffers me a shiny quarter.

"My Juliet," he says. Then he rolls over and takes a nap.

I go into the kitchen. Mammie has tuna fish ready.

"If you need anything, I could go out to the Butterfield for Jed's little steak." I'm fingering my quarter. It's enough for a cookie at Babka.

"Ye love yer sweeties," says Mammie.

My big job is cleaning Jed's ashtrays, piled high with a week's worth of butts. My favorite is a large ceramic one, about the size of a nice mince pie. I empty the pile of butts and daub the ashtray with Glass Wax to slowly reveal the names of all the shows

Jed Harris produced or directed on Broadway. Each show is in a different color, lettered in fancy script.

Coquette is a deep oxblood red. The Green Bay Tree, green. A Doll's House, raspberry. The Royal Family, aubergine. Ethan Frome, mustard. Dark Eyes, violet. Broadway, orange. The middle is reserved for Our Town. It's centered, so there's room underneath for the names of the cast. Our Town is chrome yellow. Each show gets a fresh squirt and a clean part of the rag. I leave Our Town for last. It's my favorite. Actually, it's the only one I know, for I saw it on television.

As the weeks roll into months, Jed tells me about each show. The Royal Family is not about Queen Elizabeth and her mother. It's about the Barrymores. The Green Bay Tree, Laurence Olivier's first Broadway show, had a "homo-six-ual" subplot, which Jed subtly featured through his brilliant direction. Coquette starred Helen Hayes, or "little Helen Brown," as Jed calls her. Uncle Vanya starred Tony Perkins's father, Osgood. Ethan Frome and A Doll's House starred Ruth Gordon, the mother of Jones Harris, their love child.

I take my break out on Jed's postage-stamp-sized balcony. He calls it the Juliet balcony. I'm trying to have a go with Macbeth. Jed says it'll educate me. I hear Jed and Mammie whispering in the kitchen.

O double, double toil and trouble; fire burn and cauldron bubble. Bang! goes the kettle. Mammie does this with the force of a blacksmith shoeing a mare.

"Well, no, Jed. We've neither the money nor the time."

I pick up "time."

To the last syllable of recorded time.

I can smell Jed's cigarettes. They're talking about me. Me. Can you beat it! Oh, I hope it's nice. Let me strain my ears.

"She sees all of Miss D.'s shows at City Center."

"I want her to see a Broadway show."

Jed wanders out to the terrace. There's barely enough room for the two of us. He thinks he's Julius Caesar, covered in that old sheet.

"Mind if I smoke?"

"Aww, Jed, even if I minded, you'd smoke."

"I'm offering it up for your sins."

"Aww, Jed, I don't have the time to commit any."

We laugh. Mammie comes in with a tea tray.

"I am in confab with your egg," says Jed. Mammie leaves and I scream laughing. I love it when Jed calls me egg.

Jed strikes a pose. The back of his hand against his forehead. His other arm pointing straight at me.

"What, you egg! Young fry of treachery!"

I repeat, "Young fry!" And we scream laughing at Shakespeare writing about fried eggs. Jed sweeps the branches of the overhanging tree with his bare arm.

"This castle hath a pleasant seat," he says. "The air nimbly and sweetly recommends itself unto our gentle senses."

I stand and wave my freckled arm in the direction of Jed's. He takes it and, hands entwined, we look into the tree, an ordinary dicanthus. We're in the Forest of Arden. *Tomorrow and tomorrow, and tomorrow, creeps in this petty pace from day to day.* Why is that? Tell me why, Jed. You must know. You know everything.

Jed is silent. He flicks his cigarette butt over the balcony.

Still he is silent. Lights up a fresh Salem. The Earl Grey is getting cold. Jed seductively pauses. The Harris pause. His fingers splay against his face, hiding it like a fan. He's thinking. His eyes narrow like a turtle's. I wait to hear his words punctuated by draws on his cigarette. Maybe he'll spin a series of smoke rings just for me. Me! Excitement's mounting. I'm watching Jed Harris take a deep drag on a cigarette. He makes it look delicious.

"Someday I'll tell you how I created Broadway."

And live alone in a
bee-loud glade

MAMMIE HAS BEEN WORKING FOR MISS D. a few years now, and for Jed as well. She says she still needs more in our Christmas Club to get us home to Ireland . . . *Home, Alice M'rie.* My life doesn't change much either. Every year is the same.

Autumn changes to winter. Christmas is coming, and as the days grow shorter, Mammie's workload grows larger. Not on Jed's account. He doesn't care. He doesn't celebrate. He isn't Christian. He's Jewish. "Christmas is for goyim." That's what he says. It's Miss D. who celebrates Christmas.

She gets deluged with Christmas cards. Beginning the day after Thanksgiving and continuing right up to Christmas Eve. Hundreds of them. Beautiful ones. Non-Catholic Christmas cards that don't come twenty to a box. No pictures of Jesus on a bed of goppy straw here. No St. Joseph peering over the manger. None of that dreary stuff.

Miss D.'s Christmas cards are edged in gilt and have imprinted return addresses. They don't benefit the Propagation of the Faith or the Maryknoll Missions. Miss D.'s cards promise a roaring fire, hot toddies, plum puddings, and presents galore. Miss D.'s cards come from the Metropolitan Museum, the Museum of Modern Art, Tiffany's, and Cartier.

Every morning Mammie brings in the cards on a silver tray, with a silver penknife, for Miss D. to open with her tea. Carefully. Tearing open the envelope would hint of a hasty heart. Oh, the luxury of it all. The ease. Each card more beautiful than the next. No need to race through to find the pick of the litter.

The Savoy in London sends a card the size of a menu showing a pink-and-green helium balloon sailing over the Thames. "Merrie Christmas from the Savoy!" proclaims a sprightly woman, looking suspiciously like Gertrude Lawrence. The Savoy's card vies in my heart with Dina Merrill's.

Dina Merrill. I saw her once through the porthole in the kitchen door. Dina, not named for a saint, but for the Goddess of the Hunt. Blond Goddess Dina, who looks like she's never eaten a steak in her life. Miss D. says Miss Dina's so talented, she designs her cards herself. Oh, were I that talented. If only I had the flair to make my hand curve a *D* just so. Or make an *M* look like a word in itself. If only I had the proper pen and ink to do so.

Affectionately, Dina Merrill—
(with a dash).

By the feast of the Immaculate Conception on the eighth, Christmas presents start arriving by messenger. Every year Miss D. gets a large box and a large card from

117

"21." It always says the same thing: "Love, Jack & Charlie of '21.'" All it is, mind, is an old scarf with 21's all over the place. Every year it's the same scarf, in a different design and color, screaming "21," "21," "21." I can't imagine getting the same old thing year after year and being happy about it. Yet Miss D. is. "O Big Alice," she says, "this one is even nicer than last year's." If Miss D. sits at "21"'s corner table every day, chowing down calf's liver (as Mammie says she does), why does she just get a scarf? That's what I want to know.

But Mammie's impressed. "21" is swank. "21" has statues of Negro jockeys lining their steps. And "21" (always with quote marks) has a bowl of hard candies by the door so customers can have something sweet to suck on as they ride home in their Caddies. Miss D. takes fistfuls of sweets and puts them in her bag. Then Homer gets them. Then Mammie. Even Carey likes the sweets from "21."

"Er . . . Al," he says, breaking the silence, "do ye have any of them sweeties?"

But Miss D. never uses the scarves. They remain wrapped in their tissue paper in her dresser.

Not to be outshone by Jack and Charlie, other offerings arrive. Red boxes from Cartier. Aquamarine ones from Tiffany's. Silver boxes from Bergdorf's. Oh, to have money to spend on these silver boxes, crosshatched with moss-green ribbon and tied together with a red rose. Then come the baskets of cheer. Can you beat it? Baskets of cheer.

118

All this is preamble to the Christmas tree, the Jean Dalrymple very special Christmas tree that's not green. It's white. It's artificial. That's what makes it wonderful. Around December 12, Mammie and I get the Christmas tree from its box in the cellar and assemble it.

I insert the branches in zigzag fashion into the brown crepe paper–wrapped trunk. Homer does the lights. Blue lights only. Mother Mary blue. Blue lights on an artificial white tree. Strewn through it are silver and blue balls. Just a few, mind. No other colors are allowed. When the tree's assembled, Mammie, Homer, and I place it on the mahogany table by the front window, where it catches the Fifty-fifth Street lamplight.

It is a Thursday evening. There's a light December rain falling. In the early twilight, I leave the house and cross the street to view the Christmas tree in the window. I see Mammie and Homer moving it around, getting it in exactly the right position. Mammie's pushing the tree to the left, Homer to the right.

I know what he's saying. "Big Alice," he says, "symmetrical is not chic. Slightly off center makes the statement."

The evening's not too cold, so I play my favorite game. I dash down to the Central Synagogue on Lexington and then leisurely walk back to the house. Fifty-fifth Street is a sleepy block with stately homes framed by big sheets of flagstone. Little lights signal doorways. Caddies with uniformed drivers wait by the

119

curb. Fir trees in stone planters flank entrances. Huge Norway maples, on both sides of the street, provide an overhanging canopy of branches. I stroll, mind you, stroll along, pretending I'm out on an evening's promenade.

As I approach 110, I pretend to be surprised. Oh, what a beautiful house! This is the most wonderful Christmas tree I've ever seen. It's beckoning me in. From across the street, I see Miss D. leave the house for the evening. I hang back and watch her enter the car. Miss D.'s wearing her little mink (Jed calls me his "little minx") and the littlest heels, attached to the tiniest suede shoes you've ever seen.

She's wearing one of her ribboned hats. Mammie says Miss D. has these special hats handwoven by an old granny who has nothing else to do but make Miss D.'s hats. She has hundreds of them, all the same, in every color of the rainbow, and all made of ribbon. All designed to cover her head like a wimple, yet preserve the preciseness of her long honey hair gathered up in a chignon.

I stand across the street and look at Jean Dalrymple's tree glittering in the window on a mid-December evening. Jean Dalrymple is the very essence of all that is glamorous, rich, and beautiful. I think, Someday I'll own this town house. And I'll have a blue and silver and white Christmas tree. I'll eat calf's liver on Friday. And commit adultery. And I'll send back any scarf sent from a restaurant called "21." I want presents in boxes so big I'll need a butler to carry them.

Then we rush back to get ready for another hateful Christmas in Astoria.

It's a Saturday night the week before Christmas. The phone rings. Carey makes a dash.

"Hellew, dare," he says, effecting his fakey high-pitched voice. (Years after Mammie died, he'd call me at all hours of the night, say this, and hang up.)

It's the Murphys, the Landed-Gentry-Lace-Curtain-Irish couple Mammie worked for before she married Carey.

As Mammie tells the tale, poor Peter Murphy was a widower with two small chislers, who married a career woman who worked for Gimbel's. By hiring my mammie to take care of the orphans ("O Alice M'rie, it's a terrible thing to lose yer mother"), he had the best of both worlds. A career woman for a wife. An Irish woman for a house-keeper.

The Murphys are coming all the way from Long Island to see "the Great D.D." Out comes the Dubonnet for Elizabeth. No Liz here, but the whole four syllables. Out comes the Four Roses for Carey and Pete. *Bang!* goes the kettle for Mammie and me.

"Daddy, can we put on the tree?"

"Ee'ra, it'll burn the place down."

"It won't. The lights have the Good Housekeeping Seal of Approval."

Bang! goes Carey's hand across my face.

"That'll teach ye to back talk."

121

The bell rings. I'm in the bathroom adjusting my stiff upper lip, splashing freezing water on my face. Mammie goes downstairs to greet the Murphys.

"Where's the Great D.D.?" Elizabeth bellows. She's wearing a mink coat bigger than Miss D.'s.

"Darling!" says Carey, imitating me and giving her a big kiss.

Bastard, I think, coming out of the bathroom, my stiff lip firmly in place.

The Murphys bear gifts, all dressed in red 'n' white candy-stripe glossy paper from Gimbel's. Déclassé is what Mammie's thinking. Pretty is what I'm thinking. Elizabeth may be a brassy dame with a hollow leg, but without fail, she always brings me a pretty dress. Pretty, mind, not grown-up, practical, or made of natural fibers. This year it's nylon, with big blue flowers and a Pilgrim lace collar. I sit on the floor with Mitzi looking at the dress. It's a dress that says, I know you are a pretty child. I sit on the floor under an unlit and underdecorated Christmas tree and listen to the palaver ricocheting across the room from couch to chair.

"Well, Pete, how're t'ings at Con Edison?" Carey asks, not bothering to wait for the answer.

"There's an old expression, you know. . . ."

"And what's that, D.D.?" Elizabeth inquires.

Old fool, she knows what he'll say. He says the same thing every year. "Well, 'tis always better to light a watt than curse the darkness."

Old reprobate. That's one of my new words. Not even lighting the tree.

"Daddy, can we turn on the Christmas tree now?"

"O D., pul-eeeze turn it on. It's on Con Edison!" says Elizabeth, wheezing into her Dubonnet.

Then Carey gets up, walks around the back of the tree where the plug is, and turns on our green Christmas tree. For a minute, mind, a minute. But that minute is beautiful. Wondrous. Magical. And you know why? Because for that minute, Carey isn't visible. He's hidden behind the tree. Carey's so afraid we'll blow a fuse and be evicted, he actually stands guard behind the tree, making sure it's lit but a scant minute.

"Denis, you're the greatest," Elizabeth honks, shaking her big, gaudy, gold, jingly charm bracelet. Jesus, if Carey's so wonderful, why don't you take him back with you to Long Island? Carey pushes a Dubonnet into Mammie's hand. She sits there pretending to sip. Sometimes she lets the ruby liquid just brush her lips, so afraid is she to drink. To get drunk. To be a drunk. She doesn't. Wouldn't. Can't. People think all the Irish are drunks.

A bouquet of Four Roses later, Carey and Pete begin to sing. The "O Ireland, you're so fabulous, it's a pity I ever left you" sort of thing. Carey does the singing, for he knows the songs. Pete does the deedle diddle do diddle dum dums.

*The pale moon was rising o'er the green
mountains.*
The sun was reclining beneath the blue sea.
*When I stayed with my love to the pure crys-
tal fountain,*
*That stands in the Bee-You-Dee-Full Vale
of Tralee.*

Mammie is blue in the face. She hates this Paddy stuff. Elizabeth is red in the face. She thinks it's the real McCoy. The genuine article. The kissing of the Blarney Stone without having to bend over and show your panties. Tears, actual tears, appear on Elizabeth's cheeks. Now I hold her in contempt. She's not 100 percent Irish. She's a pretender-to-the-throne Irish American. She's never been to Ireland in her life. The nearest she gets is listening to Jack McCarthy host the St. Patrick's Day Parade on TV. Yet it gets to her, all that crystal vale stuff.

"O D., have you ever been to Tra-lee?" bleats Elizabeth. Her lipstick is now smeared up her nose from all the boo-hooing.

"Sure, that's where we're from? Al—"

"Well, no, D.," says Mammie. She knows it's the Four Roses talking. "We're from Killarney."

"Near enough! Near enough!" screams Carey.

"We're from Carrigeen," says I.

"Where?" says Elizabeth. "Is there a song about Car-a-where?"

124

"No. But there's a monument in the town square dedicated to the Four Kerry Poets. Right, Mammie?" Mammie says nothing.

"But there isn't a song about Car-a-where, is there?" Another Four Roses is poured.

"No."

"Well, what kind of a place is it?"

I go into my room and put my new dress on my bed. Mitzi sits on it. Homer won't like it. I bet he'll think it vulgar. It is vulgar. All those gaudy blue flowers. Hydrangeas. I sit there stroking my dress. It's wonderfully pretty and blue.

Elizabeth is singing, "Come to me, my melancholy baby."

Pete says they've got to go. "It's a long drive to Long Island."

A little snow is beginning to fall. Elizabeth is down at the door. Carey's down there, too. If we've been too loud, the landlord can yell at him.

"Denis, you're the greatest," Elizabeth brays, and the door closes on another Astoria Christmas.

I hear Carey's heavy step on the stairs. He's whistling his song, the theme from *The High and the Mighty*. It's about an aeroplane pilot, Big John Wayne, willing to go down with his ship. Straight up to heaven. Dry legs in a bag, as Carey says.

It's freezing. Mammie's already in bed. She's scurried in, still with her street clothes on. Mitzi and I do the same thing. No point confronting Carey staggering into the living room. Bottles clink. He staggers against the Christmas tree. It falls. We hear it. We do nothing. There's no point. Next year the same thing'll happen again.

On Christmas Eve, Lily McCann comes by with a box of Loft's chocolate-covered cherries. This turns out to be the true sweets of sin.

Oh, what fool this mortal she, to commit a sin so low as to snatch a chocolate-covered cherry and cram it in her craw before Midnight Mass on Christmas Eve. But I do. I am so excited about getting a box of Loft's chocolate-covered cherries, I forget to keep my fast. See, to receive Holy Communion in the dark of a Christmas midnight, one can neither drink a drop nor take a bite from three in the afternoon to the Holy Hour. Now my soul glows from the sin of greed.

Up in heaven Mary looks over at Joseph with tears in her eyes and says, "Serves her right, that greedy little git, not waiting for Christmas morning."

Wait? Wait? The Careys don't wait. Chocolate-covered cherries, their hidden liqueury fondant so irresistible, cry out to be crammed in my mouth.

Later I'm sitting with Mammie, in the darkened, freezing Mac. (Carey waits for morning Mass.) Suddenly, *whoosh*—midnight. Lights blaze up. Father Lyons leads the procession of altar boys up the aisle. I can't turn to Mammie and say, Mammie, I'm sorry, I can't go to Holy Communion. I've eaten a chocolate-covered cherry.

Yet if I don't go, she'll have to walk up the aisle by herself. I'll be alone in the pew. Alone for the entire Mac to see and take notice of. My mammie will be mortified in front of Mrs. CarneyConroyLarkin. Everyone must go to Holy Communion on Christmas Eve. The Baby Jesus cries if you don't.

O mortal sin of mortality, you don't scare me at all. The sweets of sin . . . I receive the Eucharist with chocolatey morsels still hidden in my cheeks.

Life returns to normal on Boxing Day, the day after Christmas. With the *Blue Fairy Book* under my arm, I trudge into New York with Mammie to spend the day with Jed. Miss D.'s in the country for the holidays. On a timer, the wonderful blue tree will go on and off by itself.

"Little Alice, march your flat pheasant feet in here this instant."

Clump, clump, clump, go Macy's "health shoes" for extra support.

"How was Saturnalia?"

"Jed, we're Catholic, not Jewish."

"Jewish? Saturnalia stems from the Roman god Saturn. Obviously your mater hasn't reared you in the old Celtic myths. . . . Big Alice, you are lax in mythological duties toward your egg."

Jed pats the bed. I sit next to him. Through the smoke of his fag, he gives me the big-bad-wolf look and we laugh at our private joke. I love the pagan smell of

127

stale fags and Scotch. I know all about pagans from *Pagan Love Song*, starring Esther Williams and Howard Keel. Sarongs, blue lagoons, romance on the high seas. Now that I'm in mortal sin, I'm a pagan, too. I've not gone to Confession. If I die in my sleep, I'll ride the chute to hell.

"Jed, do you know what mortal sin is?"

"Darling, Catholicism is dreary. If Helen Hayes weren't Catholic, she'd be a better actress."

Mammie arrives with the tea. Jed pats the other side of the bed. She sits and pours. He continues.

"Big Alice and sweet little egg–Alice, the Roman feast of Saturnalia was celebrated in Ireland by the Celts." *Slurp, slurp. Puff, puff.* "Big Alice, did you celebrate this great feast, back when you lived in a mud hut?"

He's asking my mammie if she lived in a mud hut in Ireland. No wonder she's silent. She's offended. I'm silent. Jed's silent.

"Mammie, you know, like in the song: 'Out of many a mud-walled cabin eyes were watching—'"

"Egg, silence. I'm endeavoring to educate you both. Saturnalia was the feast of the winter solstice, where children could act like adults and give orders."

Big silence. Mammie's still thinking of that old mud hut. Maybe she did live in one. I'm thinking, Give orders? I never gave an order in my life.

"Egg, give an order." Jed Harris gives me a look. Smiles with his eyes.

"Aww, Jed, I dunno. . . ." I'm so embarrassed. Carey's the one who gives orders, and they're never nice. I take another cuppa with extra sugar for strength.

"Your mother tells me you avoid the Great White Way."

"Jed, I took my vow of purity with the other girls last—"

"Egg, the Great White Way is Broadway!"

With that, Jed Harris rears himself from the bed. He's wrapped in that old sheet with cigarette burns all over it. He begins to sing. "Don't bring a frown to old Broadway. You've got to clown on Broadway."

Then he gets a fit of coughing and collapses on the bed, gasping. Mammie rushes to the kitchen. She comes back with a bottle of Cutty Sark. "Jed, do ye want a drop?" Jed settles back under the covers.

"I invented Broadway, you know. If it wasn't for me, the song would never have been written. My first show was called *Broadway*. The marquee proclaimed, 'Jed Harris Presents *Broadway*.'" Jed gulps down a shot. "Jean and her cronies should think of me, not the Shuberts, when they rave over a show. Me! To hell with the Nederlanders and that ass Merrick and that phony Alex Cohen. Me! Me! They should think of me!"

Jed starts to cough again. Mammie gives him another Cutty, and calm is restored. Jed puts his hand on mine.

"Little Miss Alice, would you like to see a Broadway show?"

He asks ever so nicely. Carey never asks anything. It's bang this, slap that. Even Mammie doesn't ask me what I want, and I know she loves me. Polish this. Ice cube that.

"O Jed . . ." And I begin to cry.

Mammie goes into a silent huff, buttoning up her big stiff lip.

"O Jed, I'd love to see a Broadway show. I really would. And I know which one, too."

Mammie is lockjawed. I pull the *Times* out from under the bed.

"O Jed, this is what I want to see. *Peter Pan*, starring Mary Martin. I've seen the billboard on the Winter Garden Theatre: Peter flying over London through suns, moons, stars, and fairy dust."

Jed puts on his half glasses. He means business. "Now darling, you sure you want to see Mary? Alfred and Lynn are up . . . and Kit Cornell. . . ."

"Jedddd . . ."

"You're sure you're sure? Now Mary's trouble. Just because they all love her to death doesn't mean she's sweet or a good actress. I have it on very good authority Mary's a first-class cunt."

"*Jed!*" screams Mammie. "Alice M'rie doesn't know the word."

"Well, now she does."

"Jed, I want to see *Peter Pan*. It's an order."

Jed closes the *Times*.

"Done."

I start to laugh. I start to cry.

"Big Alice, get Richard Halliday on the phone. Tell him I want house seats for his wife's show, for my egg and her hen."

With that, Jed falls asleep, and Mammie and I go back to Astoria.

And i shall have some
peace there, for peace
comes dropping slow

THE DAY AFTER OUR GALA, La Greca, Geoffrey, and I leave for a pilgrimage to the holy island of Skellig Michael. We leave Cork at the "cracka" dawn and cross over the mountains to Kerry. Near Waterville, when the road cuts near the coast, we see them: two jagged shapes rising out of the Atlantic Ocean. The Skelligs. I've known about them all my life. Mammie and Father Bob always used them as place references.

I'd be in Father Bob's car looking at a road map.

"Mammie, where's Valentia?"

"Oh, out by the Skelligs."

And suddenly there they are. It seems fitting that I am going to share this experience with a man who was once a priest.

La Greca is sitting in the back of the car, cap on head, marveling that we aren't listening to Irish radio but playing show tunes. *Hello, Dolly!* and *Sweeny Todd* blast onto the Caha Mountains. There isn't a lyric Geoffrey and I don't know and don't want to bellow out to the sheep on the Healy Pass.

"This is like Fellini, you guys. *This* is like Fellini," says La Greca. And he says it over and over. Our small

134

rented car swerves past hoards of sheep, their forelocks splashed in identifying Day-Glo colors. They block the road, putting us in danger of careening down to the Atlantic.

And where's the comfort, sister? The comfort is, I'm traveling with a man who was once a priest. Even today, when I'm on a plane and I spot a priest wearing a Roman collar, an old flash of superstition pops into my head. I think if we were about to crash, he could give General Absolution to all the passengers and I'd fly right up to heaven, "dry legs in a bag." Of course, I no longer believe in heaven, nor do I go to Confession (or what they now call the Sacrament of Reconciliation). What have I to be reconciled about? Anyway . . . put it away, Alice M'rie. Throw those old wounds out the window and watch them crash into the sea.

We stop in Waterville for lunch at the Butler Arms. It's the hotel Charlie Chaplin frequented, where you can't take a pee without a picture of old Charlie smiling down from the wall at you. Geoffrey's off by the phones trying in vain to reach Dog's Body to find out why they all disappeared.

"So, listen," says La Greca, "tell me about Father Bob."

"He was my uncle; he was *just* a priest."

"A diocesan priest."

"Well, he wasn't a Jesuit." And we laugh, for La Greca once was.

"But he was the sun, the moon, and the stars to Mammie and me. We were pen pals. Wrote all the time, grown-up stuff about movies, movie stars. He thought it funny I belonged to the James Mason fan club."

"I think it's funny."

"Father Bob's hair looked like Mason's—black, wavy, lots of it. Said he never washed it. That's why it wasn't gray."

"Now you tell me," says La Greca, rubbing his hand over his shaved pate.

"I'd write to him for Irish books, and he'd send them to Astoria. *A School History of Ireland*, in two volumes, Moore's *Melodies*. I still have them. And he'd send cards with fairies and black kittens with red bows wishing me good luck on my exams. Then that summer, when Mammie took me back to Ireland, and when I looked sort of grown-up—you know, hair in a bun, blazers, and such—I guess he got a crush on me."

"That's not what we call it 'inside,'" says La Greca.

THAT SUMMER IN CARRIGEEN, Mammie'd say, "Bob's got a girlfriend." And everyone loved it. After saying his Mass at the friary on Sunday, Father Bob and I'd go walking around Killarney, hand in hand, with Mammie bringing up the rear.

When he wasn't saying Mass, he was funny. Englishy. He'd say things like "Cheerio!" and "luv" and "brolly." I even got used to his calling cigarettes fags. And he'd buy me fistfuls of sweets. Oh, those Cadbury chocolate bars of Turkish Delight.

"Alice M'rie, the Irish milk from the Irish cows that comprises the Irish Cadbury chocolate bar is superior to milk from the English cows." That's what Father Bob'd say as he stroked my hand.

But he was a stiff old Mass-sayer. He went by the book. Doe-mee-nous-vooo-bees-cummm. No fast in 'n' out at the friary. Mammie and I would avoid his Mass and go down to the cathedral for the quickie. But even as we'd kneel there with the Killarney townies, hanging over us was the promise of a special indulgence if we "heard" Father Bob's Mass and received Holy Communion from his very hand.

Mary Falvey and Dave truly believed that if the family attended Father Bob's Mass, they'd receive a special indulgence to get them immediately into heaven when they died. Mammie and I knew it was superstition, but we believed a teeny bit of it, so we'd make a few appearances at the friary when Father Bob was saying Mass there to take advantage of this indulgence. We'd grit our teeth at the smell of his old nicotine-stained fingers as he gave us Holy Communion.

After Mass we'd go to Scott's Hotel for lunch, which was an all-day affair. A table was reserved for Father Bob, ourselves, and the few invited neighbors who heard his Mass and were pleased as punch to be sharing a meal with the Father.

There were starched tents of linen napkins. Ashtrays stationed at every other seating. Soldiers of Guinness lining the center of the table. Coasters with little fauns gamboling among the stars and proclaiming O I'd Love a Baby Cham—the girls' drink. Large platters of well-cooked lamb and peas, as well as three bowls filled with three kinds of potatoes: mashed, boiled, and chipped.

Father Bob would sit next to me at the head of the table, his hand over my hand on his black pants knee. Lining up his peas on the tongs of his fork, he would hold court:

"Oh, it's a terrible thing, all the young girls killed in England today. It's the drugs, you see. Drugs, and young lads speeding around. Just the other night I was called to an accident by the roundabout at Sainsbury's. Terrible. Terrible. Raining. Bank holiday, too. The lad was dead. But he wasn't a Catholic. . . ."

"Now, Bob, how do ye know that?" chirps up Mammie, hanging on his every word.

"The girl told me. Poor thing. Died in my arms . . . her whole jugular severed."

Dave Slattery bleats, "Whist, Alice M'rie, pass the lamb."

Father Bob releases my hand, and I do. Never missing a beat, he continues.

"I bent down to give her absolution, and the poor girl, a lovely redhead, could barely speak. 'Father, Father, bless me, Father, for I have sinned.' You know . . . the

138

usual. Oh, the blood was everywhere. Joan, my house-keeper, said it took a whole box of carbolic to clean my collar. The girl was fading. 'My daughter'—I call them my daughter for the transference, you see. Alice M'rie knows all about that."

"I do?"

"Father, daughter."

Father Bob squeezes my hand again against his fat knee.

"'Tell me your confession,' I said to the poor girl.

"'O Father, impure—'

"And she died. Fast cars. Fast women. O Alice M'rie, the sixties are a terrible time to be young in. . . ."

"Oh, 'tis, Father Bob, 'tis," pipes up an old hen, hanging on his every word and passing around a tin of snuff.

"Alice M'rie," whispers Father Bob, "do you pray to the patron saint of Youth Purity, St. Maria Goretti?"

"Once in a while."

"Whist, Alice M'rie, stop hoggin' the spuds," croaks cousin D.D.

Father Bob releases my hand and I pass the spuds.

I STOPPED TALKING. The waitress is hovering. Any talk of priests and they loiter. Pedophilia is on everyone's brain.

". . . and the special today is roast lamb."

La Greca peers over his glasses.

"With potatoes?"

"Yes, sir, we have chips, boiled, and mash."

"I'll have all three."

We spend the night on Valentia, one of Ireland's most southwesterly islands, where in 1865 the first telegraph was made to Newfoundland. The next morning dawns fair, and as we approach the quay at Portmagee, "charons" and their boats—some flimsy at best—await us. But one man stands apart.

"I hope he's our boatman," says La Greca.

And you'd have to be blind not to think so yourself. Peter Mackey is the Man of Aran and the Flying Dutchman rolled together in a raggy Irish sweater. There isn't a finer boatman to be had in all of Ireland: tall, dark, handsome, with nicotine-stained fingers.

"He looks like Gabriel Byrne," says a lady.

"I'm nursing off the night," says Peter, giving me a wink.

Peter Mackey's boat holds about thirty people, all eager to be tortured. Ooooh, look at the headlands, they say. *Wow!* aren't they green. Next parish, America. People say things like that to ease their fear of fear, for they know Skellig Michael is for neither the weak nor the fainthearted. It's an all-day trek, scary as it is magnificent. Once you're there, you're stuck till the return trip.

The first half hour is a piece of cake, a cruising-down-the-river-on-a-Sunday-afternoon sort of thing. Then you leave the headlands and enter the Atlantic. This is not a mere boat ride. Considering I was coming from Fire Island, where the sea is a killer, you'd think I might have an inkling. But I haven't a clue.

In our breezy New York way, we are prepared with our sunblock, caps, chocolate bars, grapes, water, and spiffy Knopf guide to Ireland. Yet we are hardly prepared for the sight of this barren 715-foot rock mountain charging straight up from the sea, daring us to climb to its summit.

From curve of shore to bend of bay, Peter's boat rises and dips with the currents. I'm reminded of Bosch's painting of the ship of fools, for that's what we look like, hanging on for dear life with one hand and manipulating cameras with the other.

"We may get the dolphins on the way back," says Peter, fag drooping from his mouth. "No gales nor swells today. If we had them, I'd be back in the pub and yuz'd all be disappointed." Our eyeballs lock in terror. Swellingly swell swells already have us sliding like a deck of cards.

Hundreds of gannets soar above us, their home being the smaller of the two Skellig rocks, a seabird preserve. Peter eases the boat near "little" Skellig so we can poke our heads over the side and take pictures of this white mountain—white from gannet guano, which the monks dried and used for currency and fuel.

Birds swirl and swirl. Cheeky ones drop down to torpedo the boat. Others sleep on the rocks. These birds seem cool, hip. They've seen it all, for as far back as the Middle Ages people donned pilgrim dress to make this trek. And for what? To get a blessing like Mammie and I thought we'd get from Father Bob in Killarney? For the hell of it?

An hour or so later we arrive at a small stone pier covered in green sea-grassy slime. Peter helps us off, and La Greca is thrilled to be offered a sinewy arm to grasp on to. Now we're on our own. No restrooms, snack bars, or telephones, though there is a helicopter pad in case a pilgrim gets a heart attack.

No snakes, either. (Skellig Michael is named after the archangel Michael, who is said to have helped St. Patrick chase the snakes out of Ireland.) After a fairly easy walk on cement steps with people cheering, "This is nothing, you should see Croagh Patrick," there looms in front of us the thousand-year-old stone stairway of six hundred steps. You can see why the monks who came here in the sixth century thought this rock island to be the end of the world itself.

Geoffrey leads the way, and La Greca brings up the rear, with me in the middle like the cream in an Oreo cookie. It's hot. Barren. Grecian. Unlike Ireland. One minute I'm scalded by sun, the next minute the hairs on my arms are standing up from the wind. The air is sharp, every breath a needle. And it's scary. There are no guardrails, fences, or barricades to prevent me from hurling myself into the Atlantic.

I think of Carey, and how at his most venomous he would give a call from work to announce, "I'm going to Ireland and jump off the Cliffs of Moher." Mammie and I always hoped he would.

We climb up a level. Take a rest. Up another level. Take a picture. Up another. A swig of water. A daub of sunblock. Sweat drips from us. People are dropping out, returning to the concrete platform, which under the circumstances seems as comfy as a feather bed. The steps grow steeper the higher up we go; so steep I can't walk upright and have to climb on hands and knees.

The higher we get, the farther we are from the world as we know it. I become obsessed with the sun, the unrelenting sun permeating the straw brim of my hat and scalding my nose. I peek down, down to the cool, dark blue velvet of the Atlantic, with nary a Lorelei to greet me. If I jump, will I not become part of the Celtic twilight? Will I not join in spiritual communion with the monks?

Near the summit we find ourselves in a psychedelic-green glade, matted in a watercress-like vegetation (possibly dulse) the monks used for food. It's our first chance to rest in a bit of comfort. And in unison, we pilgrims take a break on the saddle, as it's called. Suspended in this green glen in the sky, people sit peeling bananas, eating Kit Kat bars, and peering up to the summit for a glimpse of the six dome-shaped stone huts where the monks lived, worked, and died.

La Greca is in heaven.

"This is fabulous! Those monks were *cra-zee!*"

They'd have to be. Monks without their morning tea. Monks chanting into the pre-light of dawn to God. Monks sweating bullets in woolly robes, in bare feet. Monks deranged from eating cress and an occasional seagull or puffin. Monks without Guinness or nary a drop of the craythur to soothe them if they were blue. Maybe they kept bees. Maybe they made mead. Did the monks not want to get drunk? Drunk, like pagans would, to worship their God? They would have to worship the sun, for it is the sun that rules Skellig Michael, not God as we know him.

The monks must have known this, for they built their beehive dwellings, and a chapel, facing west to the setting sun. The land of T'ir na Nog. The land of the dead. The land of the forever young. The reason the West Room faces west.

I get a faraway look in my eye.

"Alice Marie, are you okay?" asks La Greca.

"I'm not Alice M'rie no more."

"And she's forgotten her grammar, too."

"Sorry, the sun's addled my brains."

We proceed to the summit. If I had the strength to run, I would do so, to escape the sun for the stony cool of a beehive. We are so far up in the sky, I feel at one with the blue—a Mother Mary blue—sky, with nary a cloud in sight. Away over there, veiled in mist, is the island of

144

Ireland, where people pray for sun, never wear sunblock, and burn to death when they visit the Mediterranean. I can barely make it out.

After a few gulps of water, the taking of a potential Christmas card photo, and a few tempered exclamations of *Faaaaabulous* from La Greca, we walk around the minuscule terrace that the beehive huts are built upon. Geoffrey's writing in his diary. Tourists are reading the *Blue Guide*, taking pictures, and looking down to see if Peter Mackey's boat has come to rescue them. There is a frisson of excitement in the air. We have achieved our goal. The weather is perfect. I got us to the Skelligs. And we climbed to the top. Yet I feel strangely sad. If I had my druthers, I'd be back in New York.

Alice M'rie, I think to myself, admit it, you miss your mammie. You miss someone you don't even remember. You miss your mammie, whose voice you've all but forgotten.

It occurs to me that this summit was the place Mammie had pointed to from the *Mauretania* O those many years ago, when I was young and she was not yet old. Again, La Greca catches the faraway look in my eye. It takes a priest.

"Doll . . . tell me."

"Oh, I'm looking at Ireland over there and thinking what it was like coming back to Kerry with my mother. We saw the Skelligs from the ship. . . . Onboard everything seemed so full of promise. We had such high hopes then."

Dropping from the veils
of the morning to where
the cricket sings

ON THE MAURETANIA dawn arrived at around four-thirty in the morning. So on the day we were scheduled to land in Ireland, Mammie and I crept out of bed at four, put on our arrival outfits, and scampered upstairs to the main deck to see the dawn on the hills of Ireland.

"Mammie, it's a fine day."

And it is. A dreamy, gray-apple-green day, made sweeter with the knowledge that it could just as easily be a dark, dank, rainy one. In the chilly dawn, stewards are walking around with trays of steaming hot cups of tea, mixed with milk and sugar. In the distance is the rocky Kerry coast. I can barely make it out.

"Mammie, do you know where we are?"

"By the Skelligs. See there? See the top of that rock?"

Then she gets silent. She's looking way beyond the horizon. She's looking way, way over there. Beyond the Skelligs. Beyond Mangerton Mountain. Beyond the Lakes of Killarney.

"Mammie, what'er you looking at?"

"Oh, I'm looking Home. Home, Alice M'rie. Dave and Father Bob are just getting into the cars to meet us."

As the *Mauretania* inches near the coast, we start picking out outlines of stone cottages. First one, then another, then another would light up. Men are going out to the "haggard," or barnyard, to milk the cows. Women are putting the kettle on for tea. All over Ireland tea is being poured into cups, just as it is on deck. At that moment everyone on land and on sea is united by this wonderful drink, this balm that warms the hands as it warms the heart. This cup of tea.

Silence. Oh, the silence of all the passengers. The rich and the poor. The tourists and the Irish diaspora clutching cups in the early morning damp. Hoping, all of them. Hoping this summer'll be nice. Hoping this summer'll be warm. Hoping this summer there'll be less drink. Hoping this summer'll be less damp. Hoping. Hoping. I see it in their faces. Me too. I'm hoping the Slatterys will be glad, and I'll be glad, and Mammie'll be glad that we've finally come Home.

Tea finished, the stewards move on to passing out whiskey. Even to me. A nip in the hand to take the chill off. To warm the soul. To give courage where prayer fails. Then the singing begins. An Irish man with a melodium, a small squeeze box, begins singing "Come all ye's."

I'll take you home again, Kathleen.
Across the ocean wild and wide.

Sobbing begins.

To where your heart has ever been
Since first you were my bonny bride.

Mammie stifles back a cry. I never cry.

The roses all have left your cheeks.
I've watched them fade away and die.

Mammie's tears are hidden by her veil.

A gong sounds. Breakfast is announced. The sun pops out. The crying stops. Quick as a flash, the Irish burst into loud cries of "Oh, t'ank God we gotta fine day." Then we all sit down to a big breakfast, putting the lining in our bellies for the long day ahead.

Announcements are made to board the tender, a flat-bottom boat designed to take passengers from ship to port. *Bang!* The class system ends. Cheek by jowl, passengers from all three classes jostle. We're all going home to Ireland.

As we approach the Gothic cathedral of St. Coleman's in Cobh harbor, I get scared. Being in Ireland for six weeks may not be easy. It may deflate the starch in my dresses, the pizzazz in Mammie's hats. Mammie's going back to her family. To her people. To the Slatterys, who knew her when she was a girl. To the Slatterys, who remember her hopes and know her secrets. To people who may want her to be the way she was when she left. And she's bringing me—the fruit of her womb, Jesus.

She's bringing me. Me, with my *Hello, darling!* Alice M'rie, drop those airs. You're going to Carrigeen, a wide spot on the road to Killarney.

Mammie's gazing over to the cathedral. Do I dare take her picture? Yes, I should. It's a glamorous church. It must have beautiful weddings. I'll take a picture of Mammie in front of St. Coleman's.

"Mammie . . ."

She seems different. Yet she looks the same. There's her oatmeal dress. There's her white straw hat. There's her gloves. Yet my mammie's going through a metamorphosis. She's becoming Irish again. Irish, I tell you. Like Dark Rosaleen, Maud Gonne, Queen Maeve, and the I'll-take-you-home-again-Kathleen-girl, all rolled into one. Did this change start when she took off her gloves? Maybe when she lifted the veil off her face for a minute to get a better view of St. Coleman's? Maybe it started when the man with the melodium began playing war songs.

We'll meet again, don't know where, don't know when.
But I know we'll meet again some sunny day.

First class and third class are singing together. Mammie is singing along heartily.

As the tender approaches the dock, we can see Irish people waving at us. They all look so dour. Tweeds, caps, jackets, dark, dark, dark. Mammie and I look like

151

Christmas trees. The man with the melodium starts playing Irish songs again, and all the Irish begin to cry. Again. I feel a part of it all, yet a stranger to it all. My head is spinning. I am Little Alice, the little maid. And Alice M'rie. And Alice Carey. I don't know who I want to be here.

Mammie spots her brother Dave on the dock. She's waving madly.

"Dave! Dave! We're here!"

She's completely Irish now. And me? I'm . . . Irish American. No, I'm not at all like those Americans eager to wear green, kiss the Blarney Stone, and soak up the culture. I'm a New Yorker. And I'm Irish. Just like Mammie.

Alice M'rie, leave your airs on the tender. For the next six weeks you'll be Irish. That's what you want to be. The real article. Just like Mammie. Right?

There midnight's all
a glimmer

STANDING ON THE DOCK IN A STRAIGHT line are the Slatterys. Father Bob is in clerical black, his long, shiny, patent-leather hair severely parted in the middle, like Dagwood Bumstead's. Next to him, his brother, grizzled old Dave in his battered tweed cap. Then a little apart, hands clasped behind his back, my cousin D.D. (heir apparent to the farm) in his worn rugby blazer with gold crest. All of them smoking Sweet Aftons through nicotine-stained fingers.

Father Bob (for that's what I call him, never Bob, or Uncle Bob) whisks us through customs, in that cool and breezy way Irish priests have. The customs men part the Red Sea for us, hoping—indeed, knowing—they'll be nearer to God for the favor.

Two small black cars await our trunks, a Victrola, and the presents we've brought with us. We're laden down with summer shirts for Dave; striped ties for D.D. and his brother, Robert; and "full-figure" blouses for Mary Falvey. Mammie goes in a car with Dave and D.D. I'm in the other with Father Bob.

"Well then, Alice M'rie, how 'bout a fag?" Father Bob lights up an Afton and lets it fall to the side of his mouth.

"Ah, no, Father Bob, it's bad for the complexion."

"It's yet to ruin Grace Kelly's. She smokes like an engine."

We carry on. Banter, you know. What I'm good at. Being pen pals, we don't have much to fill in. I don't tell him that among Miss D.'s office boys, *fag*'s a loaded word. I do tell him I'm in love with James Mason.

We're on our way to Cork City for a drink and a bite at the Metropole Hotel. The lads'er dying of thirst.

"Ah, Father Bob," coos the barmaid, "ye're back for the summer *again*. May it be a fine one, please God. Why, is that the girl? Isn't she nice and big!"

I settle back with my Orange Squash, knowing this, too, will pass. Women like her talk that way. The lassie continues, "Is she going to be a nun?" Be polite, Alice. She's only a barmaid sucking up to a priest. Doesn't she see I'll be a star? She'd know if she'd seen me do my Carol Channing. Aw, but then, she wouldn't know Carol Channing if she fell on her.

"No, Eily," I say, reading her name tag, "I don't think God's calling me."

"Not yet," says Father Bob, pulling my ponytail and tucking into his pint.

The drive to Carrigeen is long and flat. I'm tired, and Father Bob's woozy from the Guinness. We switch on a radio call-in show.

"And now, a very special birthday greeting for a Mrs. Bridey Joyce way out there in Ougterguard, from her son stationed up in Derry. Here's 'They're Cutting the Corn in Creashlough Today' sung by the lovely Ruby Murray. Take it away, Ruby. Ah, it's a grand day to be cutting the corn, or the turf, or even corners, for all you working girls out there."

After a summer of this, I'll be crying for Tony Bennett.

I dangle my arm outside the car window and let the breeze run through my fingers. The Kerry mountains are in the distance. The cows are standing up. It'll be a fine day. Father Bob has already proclaimed that the heat's killin' him. 'Course, he hasn't taken off his worsted jacket. Up ahead I see our steamer trunks strapped onto Dave's car. I can hear Mammie's laugh. She's Home.

"Ah, Alice M'rie, it's nice yourself and Alice are Home."

"Oh, yes, Father Bob, it's nice to be Home."

Lie!

Carrigeen isn't my Home. My Home is Manhattan. My Home is on the East Side, where there are lovely private houses with blue morning glories twined round the railings. My Home is the Beverly coffee shop, where I languish over a chocolate malt and a tuna down. (Extra mayo, please.) My Home is the floor of Miss D.'s office. My Home is Central Park in the snow. My Home is Jed's bedroom. My Home isn't Astoria or Carrigeen. My Home is all those places I want to be my Home.

The Paps come into view. Then the fields, the cows, and the house. A just-built two-story stucco house, plopped by the side of the road, painted dove gray with a peach trim. Smack up against it is the house Mammie calls Home. The old house of her childhood. Once thatched, now tinned and used as a cow barn. In the doorway of the bungalow stands Mary Falvey, flyswatter in hefty hand.

I take a gander at her eye. Mary Falvey has one scad eye that looks up to the heavens, away from you. Her good eye stares right at you in a round, unblinking gaze, then darts away. Mary Falvey does not drive a car. This must be the reason why.

Behind Mary Falvey's head dangles a large twirl of flypaper covered with blue bottles. One of the first things Mammie does when we go into Killarney is to buy several rolls of fresh flypaper.

"O Alish M'rie, aren't ye fine and big."

Fine? Big? What is this woman insinuating?

Fine? It must be my blazer, with its lovely crest signifying nothing. And *big*? Tall, she must mean tall. But I'm short. Terrible thing to be short. Onstage I'll be tall. Just like Mary Martin. Jed says Mary makes all sorts of people believe she's tall by thinking tall. Does Mary Falvey mean *fat*, then? Not me. Not fat. Never. I'll swear off sweeties. I'll never darken a bakery's door again.

My cousin Robert, D.D.'s younger brother, ambles out. He, too, is wearing a worn blazer, but without a crest. I notice he's got a few gray hairs. Mammie's gray, too. And Carey. Maybe it runs in the family. But I'll never be gray. I'll listen to Father Bob.

"That's the secret, Alice M'rie: Never wash your hair. Just grease it up. Preserves the color."

The house is damp for July, despite a fire in the scullery fireplace that's kept going night and day and is lit by our own cut turf from the bog. A bloke called the Bogman has just been found up north, perfectly preserved in the compacted mire called "bog" that provides fuel for all Ireland. He was black haired and prehistoric and died with yellow buttercups in his mouth.

"Mind ye, Alice M'rie, er the Bogman'll get ye," Dave says, and everyone laughs as I go out to the shed for a load of stacked turf. Part of me believes him.

Guinness all around. And tea. And a new bottle of Paddy. For a good twenty minutes, we just stand there on the cement floor in the kitchen with our coats on. Dave has a swig of Paddy.

"Best whish-key in Ireland," he says. "Paddy is the daddy of them all." We all laugh. Mammie says, "O Dave, say it again." And he does.

I'm tucking into a large cup of the nicest, strongest, sweetest tea in the world and a Cadbury bar. There's so much to say, yet there's nothing to say. Mammie and Mary Falvey review the roll call of who died recently. Father Bob and Dave are deep into a silent smoking session with Sweet Afton. I'm not sure they like each other, Bob being a priest and Dave being just a farmer. Smoke covers up the awkwardness between them.

I concentrate on the large portrait of the Sacred Heart of Jesus, with its perpetually lit red votive light, prominently displayed over the kitchen table. Jesus is not calling me, no matter what Eily, the barmaid, thinks. He'd better not.

But hadn't Mollie, Mammie's sister, the one who lived in a cloister in Sherwood Forest, worn out her knees praying that I'd become a nun? That was before she died of leukemia, mind. Anyway, if she prayed so much, why did she get leukemia?

I'm tired. Mammie's tired. It's damp, and we're hungry. We decide to settle in before the evening meal. Our bellies're stuck to our backs with hunger. Mary Falvey starts cleaning some newly dug-up potatoes in a basin of bog water. Mammie and I go upstairs. We're sleeping together in Mary and Dave's room.

I unpack my talismans and put them on the night table. I line up my framed picture of Mitzi. A snap of Jed in a hammock. My diary. My pen. The small bottle of Diorissimo that Homer gave me. I lean my records against the table. *Oklahoma* broke. Mammie has nothing but reading glasses, her crime stories from the *Daily News*, and a pocket pack of Kleenex on her side. She doesn't have a picture of Carey.

Mammie and I don't know the word "casual." We don't have a casual bone in our bodies. Yet you'd think

159

we'd loosen up a bit here on the farm: a pair of slacks for her, maybe jeans for me. But ladies don't wear trousers. Mammie changes from her stylish dress into a black skirt and gray square-necked merino sweater with pearls. Pearls! Can you beat it? She takes off her hat, a concession. I put on a plaid skirt and navy sweater. I'm freezing.

We haven't gone to the bathroom since the Metropole. Mammie looks under the bed for the dreaded chamber pot, the "po." Out comes the Kleenex and down we squat. Terrible. My period has arrived. But we don't talk about things like that. In my suitcase are three boxes of Modess. Next to them, a special white cotton panty, with rubber crotch liner. This is to prevent a thin line of red on a white dress.

Modess . . . because, hiss the magazines. All those beautiful women in satin evening gowns. Oh so happy to be bleeding into a Modess. *Because* . . . I don't know if Mammie's still bleeding. She could be. She looks young. Then again, maybe not. We don't share girl stuff like that. *Modess . . . because . . .*

James Joyce named his collection of poems *Chamber Music* because he loved listening to his love, his companion, his Nora Barnacle, tinkle into their chamber pot. What did Nora do with her sanitary napkins in Trieste? Did she burn them in the fire when Jimmy's back was turned, as Mammie burns mine? Do all mothers burn their daughters' menstrual blood when the men are out?

"The men're out. We'll do it now."

160

We wash our faces in a nineteenth-century basin filled with freezing brown bog water. Good for the complexion, says Mammie. The smell of boiled potatoes mixed with Sweet Afton wafts up the stairs, and Mammie and I go down to dinner.

Each day is like the other on the Slatterys' dairy farm. No matter what the day, occasion, or holiday, Slattery cows are milked by hand by 5 A.M. Then the milk is driven by horse cart to the Killarney creamery.

Dawn is breaking over the Paps. Mammie and I are lying in bed. This is what we hear:

"D.D., get up . . . get up, I say . . . D.D. . . ."

This is the Ballad of Mary Falvey. But her accent sounds like this:

Dayyyyyy-deeee!

Git up.

Git up, oi shayyyyyy.

Mary Falvey never varies her lines. And D.D. never gets up till the ballad's repeated many, many times. Occasionally Dave chirps in with a "Whist, Day-Dee . . . listen to eer muther." But D.D. remains asleep, only to wake when Mary Falvey gets to her feet, marches into the room, and rattles his bed.

I try to go back to sleep, but I'm smothered under the weight of a quilt so heavily stuffed with cotton batten and crosshatched with stitches and buttons, it's practically impossible to turn over. Next door, we hear Father Bob snoring away. Nothing wakes him.

After a day or two, Father Bob starts coming into our room in the morning. We don't mind at all. We're so relieved not to see Carey's face. And, after all, he's a priest. Priests do what they like. Father Bob's holding out the promise of a trip to London to us. But before London, we would have to go to Liverpool and visit the small parish in Bootle where he's just been awarded his first pastorate. Liver-Pool sounds pretty grim to me.

"O Bob, yer first church. Alice M'rie's so excited to see it."

(I'm not.)

"Now, Bob, ye're at Our Lady of . . . where?"

"Walsingham."

"Oh, yes. Isn't that where the royal family stay?"

"That's Windsor, Alice."

So we put up with his early morning appearances. The door opens, and there's Father Bob, large and resplendent in his bottle-green damask bathrobe with black tassels.

"Well then, Alice, it's a fine day to be up and about. Alice M'rie, no dreaming of James Mason now."

Mammie and I don't respond to his chitchat and pretend to be sleeping. We breathe a sigh of relief when he bounds downstairs all fired up to consume a breakfast of three fried eggs, four rashers, four sausages, a healthy slice of blood pudding, several pieces of brown bread slathered with butter and marmalade, and an entire pot of tea so strong you can stand a spoon up in it.

Mammie can't drive, so we're dependent on Father Bob to go into Killarney, or "town," as we call it. There's a daily bus at eleven-thirty, returning at three-thirty, but Mammie thinks using public transportation to visit her own town is déclassé. So we pray for Father Bob to suggest a trip, which insures our making a day, and sometimes a night, of it.

Killarney *is* Ireland to me, for it's the only town I know. Dublin, four hours away by rail, is spoken about as a distant metropolis, with movie theaters, department stores, and restaurants. Killarney has none of these. And it's not pretty. But it is a town, and it's all we have. I live to go there. Mammie constantly emphasizes, "Killarney is only five miles from home," as if that makes a difference. With Father Bob's driving, it takes us a half hour to get there. If a lorry lunged, we'd be dead from his poor reflexes.

Putt . . . putt . . . putt . . .

"A lorry, Bob, a lorry!"

Screeeeeech! The car stalls.

Hand on the stick shift, Father Bob exclaims: "Oh dear . . . oh my . . . oh goodness . . . oh gracious . . . oh mercy me."

If really challenged, Father Bob gives out with a "Jesus, Mary, and St. Joseph!" You think he'd say, "Oh shite, oh shite, oh piss, oh feck," and be done with it. But no. His incompetence is aided by Mammie's unflagging support.

163

"Oh, I love driving with Bob. He goes so lovely and slow." This is the man who's going to show us London!

Anyway, when we get to Killarney, Father Bob makes a beeline to Scott's Hotel for a few jorums of Guinness, and Mammie and I walk the streets. As inveterate New Yorkers, used to change, we expect Killarney to change as well. But just as the Ballad of Mary Falvey never changes, neither does Killarney. The same pink-and-yellow *gateaux*, striped bull's-eyes, and hard-boiled sweets hang around for years in shop windows. The same cans of Batchelors mushy peas fade from green to gray in the groceries. And the same Jaffa oranges shrivel with age at the vegetable stands.

Our first stop is the butcher. Mammie and I love our butchers: sometimes seeing a fresh chicken eviscerated right before my eyes is the high point of my day.

"Ah, Miss, this chicken was sayin' his prayers this morning."

"O Pat, have ye a few lovely chops for us today?" That's what Mammie asks. Pat's chops have never been referred to as "lovely" before or since.

Then on to the paper shop, called the Favourite. Of course, they're saving the *London Sunday Times* for us.

"Th' girl's mad f'r reading."

We weave through the lanes. Hello, cobbler. Hello, baker. Outside of a faded-grandeur hotel called the Imperial, Mammie tells of a cousin, a Miss Marie Slattery, who owned it oh so long ago and cheated the Slatterys out of their rightful inheritance. The turn of the century seems as real to Mammie as yesterday, so we never go in.

It's hard navigating cobbled streets in my new patent-leather shoes with their two-inch heels. (Dave calls them thrup'ny-bit heels.) If Mammie and I need a sit-down, depending on the side of town we wind up on, we go to the friary or the cathedral. Killarney has both. Father Bob says his obligatory Sunday Mass at the friary, but it's considered unfashionable, so we spend little time there. Mammie loves the cathedral, where the Killarney elite gather for a Mass that they always come late to and leave early from—in before the Gospel, out after the Eucharist. Father Bob says it's not a sin.

Mammie and I walk around this Gothic horror, with its life-sized Stations of the Cross, pretending we're having a good time. What we're really doing is killing time. Mammie must be as bored as I with the slow pace of Killarney. I'm holding out for London, where we'll stroll down Piccadilly in the bright morning air.

After a quick prayer for poor Mollie's soul and Father Bob's "intentions," Mammie and I visit cousins, the Sullivans, for they have a bathroom. And it's at the Sullivans that I find a boyfriend. Now believe me, Haulie was no James Mason. But he had the brains to pay me a compliment that still makes me smile.

Nothing serious, mind. Haulie's religious. He sticks by the "Temperance Pledge" he took at Confirmation and proudly wears the pledge pin of Jesus's bleeding heart, gleaming from his lapel. He drinks ginger ale, doesn't smoke, doesn't dance. He doesn't know who Julie Andrews is, or Mary Martin. He reads only *The Kerryman* and *Messenger of the Sacred Heart*. And he has jug ears and big white teeth. But 'twas Haulie who paid attention to me. 'Twas Haulie who gladdened my heart as we walked back to the Sullivans' that night after the bazaar.

It's a lingering July twilight. We're on our way hack to the car—Mammie, Father Bob, the Sullivans, and me. Haulie and I are lagging behind, laughing at the crickets chirping.

"O Alice M'rie, dat's dem a'right, rubbin' d'legs together."

The sun's long pink fingers guide our way as the words pop into my head:

> *I was a child and he was a child*
> *In that kingdom by the sea*
> *And we loved with a love that was more than a love*
> *I and my Annabel Lee.*

"Go on, then, Alice M'rie. Say it again." And I did. Haulie thought I wrote it. He thought I wrote "Annabell Lee." And I let him think so.

"Ah, Alice M'rie, ye're d'real article. That's what ye are. Ye're d'real article."

That's what Haulie said. And I loved it. I loved him for saying it. I overlooked that he was no James

Mason, and we held hands. But Father Bob saw us and wanted to hold my hand as well.

DAYS AND NIGHTS FLOW TOGETHER, beginning with Mary Falvey's Ballad and ending in a haze of Sweet Afton. No date's been chosen for our visit to London. Mammie doesn't really care. She'd like to see Father Bob's splendid new church. But she can live without seeing Harrods. Her days are spent at the kitchen table, tracing relatives with Mary Falvey and drinking hundreds of cups of tea.

"Oh yes, the Nagles of Blackwater . . . that's why Mollie became a nun." Mammie starts to sniffle. Reaches for her pocket pack of Kleenex.

"Ye'd have loved her, Alice M'rie."

It's raining. We aren't going to Killarney today.

"Why did Aunt Mollie become a nun?"

"Because of Nanno Nagle. Haven't I told ye, Alice M'rie? We're related to a saint."

Father Bob strolls in. "I say, Alice, Nanno isn't a saint yet. She's up for Beatification."

Now, with any talk of saints, my ears perk up. Isn't my favorite book, next to *Theatre World*, the *Penguin Dictionary of the Saints*? Oh, the gory mess of it all. Lady saints like St. Barbara, who got her breasts lopped off. *Whack!* Or St. Catherine, strapped to that fiery wheel and twirled round and round till she dropped dead. *Plop!*

167

Mammie says Nanno Nagle founded an order of teaching nuns called the Irish Presentation Sisters. Boring.

If it were up to me, only people who suffered horrible, bone-crushing, screaming deaths would be saints. Founding an order of nuns doesn't cut the mustard. If Mammie's sister Mollie became a nun because of this other nun, no wonder they think me odd not being all fired up about it. They want me to dance down the road with Nanno and become a nun as well.

Mammie gets out a pad and starts to list all the nuns of the Slattery family.

"Now, there's Eily and Kate in Texas. And Mother Mary Columcille in South Africa . . ."

"And on the male side, Alice, let's not forget who says Mass. We have yours truly . . . and Dan Joe."

"But Bob,"—it kills me when she calls him Bob—"Dan Joe left the priesthood."

"Ah yes, Alice, but once a priest, always a priest. And our Alice M'rie one day . . . eh, Alice?" And he rubs the back of my neck.

Wink. Wink. Laugh. Laugh. *Bang!* goes the kettle. Out comes a fresh pack o' fags. This constant rain is driving me nuts. Oh, the conspiracy of the three of them. Look at them wearing out the oilcloth with their elbows. Father Bob collared up, always ready for an Extreme Unction, that one. Mammie in her hat, telling Mary Falvey she wears hats in the house because of the damp. Here come the snapshots. Mary Falvey produces an old bag chockablock with the past.

Mammie and Father Bob are eating them up.

Mammie (all teary): "It's a grand thing . . . Mollie . . ."

Father Bob (lighting a fag): "All these women sacrificing their personal lives."

Mammie (looking at a picture of Mollie): "Oh, 'tis."

Father Bob (blowing a smoke ring): "Indeed."

Mammie (prodding her finger in my back to let me know I slouch): "The nuns in Astoria tell Alice M'rie—"

Father Bob (grabbing my hand): "—that God is—"

Mammie (prodding again): "—calling her."

Father Bob (letting my hand go): "O Alice M'rie, you didn't write me that. Tell us now."

"O Mammie, I don't remember."

We aren't making any moves toward London. The smoke from Sweet Afton drives me out to the yard. There is no place to go. There is nothing to see. Just a few smelly cows. An old pig wallowing in mud. And some chickens. I could go upstairs and play *South Pacific*. That always cheers me up. But it won't work now. Conspirators, that's what they are. I bet Mammie and Father Bob want to get me into the convent this summer. Maybe in London. Maybe in Sherwood Forest, near Mollie's convent. While I'm standing there, looking at Mollie's grave, those nuns'll kidnap me. Slap a black veil on my head.

Father Bob comes out of the house.

"O Alice M'rie, I fear we said the wrong thing. Your mother and I, we were just joking. Having a daughter a nun is a great assurance for a mother."

169

"'Tis."

"Alice tells me this Mr. Harris has a special relationship with you."

Jed! She couldn't have started in on Jed.

"Jed's fine. He wants to educate me."

It starts to rain again. We move toward the old house. It's spooky, full of chicken feathers and a few old tractors.

"Alice says you sit on his bed. Do you hold hands?"

"No! Jesus, Bob!"

I call him Bob without the "Father."

"There's no place else to sit. I don't go near him. He smokes."

"So do I."

With that, Mammie shouts that the tea's boiling and we should come in for a cup.

And noon a purple glow

FATHER BOB FINALLY SETS THE DATE and we are on our way to England. What he wants to do is drive up to Dublin on Wednesday morning and take the Channel boat across the Irish Sea that night. This'll get us to Liverpool on Thursday, where we'll stay through the weekend. We'll see his church, watch him say Mass, take advantage of that "special indulgence." Then we'll take the train down to London on Monday.

Homer sends me a list of to-do's he's thought up for Mammie and me. In London we must go to the Ritz for tea and cucumber sandwiches. We must go to Harrods and say hello to the teddy bears for him. Then I must go to Floris on Jermyn Street and buy myself a big bottle of eau d'cologne. He even sends me a traveler's check to pay for it.

Homer says that just because Father Bob wears black does not mean he has taste.

The Channel boat is not nearly as glamorous as the *Mauretania.* It's packed to the gills with people smoking and drinking. Father Bob doesn't spring for a cabin. He's quite happy to sit up in the bar all night. Mammie and I have no recourse but to settle down in the lounge area. We eat Digestive Biscuits and drink tea. Then Mammie crumples up on a bench and falls asleep. I'm not sleepy, so I go out on deck and look into the dark. I'm so excited to be sailing to the land of William Shakespeare, Noël Coward, and the Queen.

The moment the dock comes into view I see that Liverpool is not nice. Mammie says it isn't yet fully recovered from being bombed in the War. On the drive to Bootle, all we see is vacant lot after vacant lot, full of crumbling bricks, scrawny wallflowers, and stray dogs.

Then suddenly there it is. In the middle of a corner vacant lot stands a green Quonset hut with a large sign proclaiming OUR LADY OF WALSINGHAM.

Mammie's in shock.

"Green, eh, Alice? For Ireland," says Father Bob.

"Yes," says Mammie.

"No Union Jack here," says Father Bob.

The presbytery's worse. In Carrigeen, all Father Bob could talk about was his smashing new house. Can't he see this is a poky two-up/two-down row house? In Bootle! Bootle, f'r God's sake.

"Near the racetrack. The Grand National, eh, Alice?" says Father Bob, happy as a clam. But Bootle isn't Liverpool, and Liverpool isn't England. Only London is England. We're trapped.

We're trapped here, and that's the truth. Mammie and me with hefty old Joan, Father Bob's Cockney housekeeper. She greets us at the door, squeezes Mammie, and calls me "ducky." *Bang!* goes the kettle. Out come the biscuits. Welcome to England.

Mammie and Joan are thicker than thieves. They're Father Bob's self-appointed handmaidens. What's worse is they're happy. Happy to be divvying up duties they'll perform for the nearest thing they have to God. Joan does his laundry. "Missus, I know m'starch. That I do, lass." Mammie makes his bed and tidies his room.

We go back and forth to the church several times a day. Each time Father Bob has some new revelation he wants to share with us.

"Why, Alice M'rie, here's a surprise for you. I'll bet you don't know who Our Lady has as a parishioner?" I say nothing, and Father Bob says, "George Harrison's mother, that's who we have. I've met George. He's a good boy." Then Mammie says: "Who's George Harrison, Bob? Is he Rex's son?"

There are no statues in the church, but around the walls are Stations of the Cross. In the middle are about fifty folding chairs. That's it. Father Bob doesn't seem to mind. Yet Jesus is living in Father Bob's Quonset hut. The red light is on day and night saying, He's there in his gold tabernacle. But instead of residing on a marble altar, Jesus of Bootle is living on an old kitchen table covered with a white cloth. That kills Mammie.

Father Bob goes on, "We're having a bazaar to get a proper altar. Mrs. Harrison said George might contribute something. Maybe he could come by and sing us a few songs like 'I Wanna Hold Your Hand.'"

"But Bob," says Mammie, "why have you no electricity?"

"We don't need any. We do all our services in daylight."

"Even Christmas?" say I.

"We haven't had a Christmas yet," says Father Bob.

That finished, there's nothing left to say. We go round the corner to buy a piece of beef, a few spuds and onions, a cabbage, and a kidney. Joan is going to make a Lancashire Hot Pot.

On Saturday morning we clean out Father Bob's study. It's a smelly old place. Ashtrays piled with butts. Old socks. Pomade. Whiskey. Sweat. Mammie lures me in with the promise of some pictures of India that Father Bob took when he was a chaplain there during the War. I have to cooperate or they'll think me cranky.

Mammie gets up on a chair to start tidying the top shelves of the bookcase. Raymond Chandler, *Quo Vadis*, *The Silver Chalice*, *Irish Bar Room Jokes*. Real junk. She's worried Father Bob'll come back and find us rummaging about. But Joan says he's gone for the day. Then she says (and this just kills me), "Alice M'rie, why don't you go to Confession to your uncle. I'm sure he wouldn't be hard on the sins of a young girl." And they both laugh at me.

I pay them no mind. I stay looking at the snaps from India. To my surprise, there are lots of pictures of a pretty Indian lady standing with Father Bob. In front of a chapel. In a jeep. And in front of the Taj Majal. His arm is always around her. She's wearing a sari. He's in RAF khakis without his Roman collar. He's younger. Thinner. Smoking. Same black hair, parted in the middle.

"Aren't they wonderful pictures?" says Mammie.

"Oh yes," says Joan. "He has that fine woman with him."

Mammie gets down off the chair and bends down to see. Then she takes the box of snaps, puts it back, and says, "Well, that's enough. Bob can't expect us to look after him. He's messy."

"That he is," says Joan.

"He'll have to live with his mess," says Mammie.

"Let's have a cup of tea," says Joan. And we do.

And that's the truth. But there's more. More, I tell you. The Quonset hut does Mammie in. It's not what she'd wanted for Father Bob. She's up most of that night sitting at the window, reading her crime pages by lamplight. When morning rolls around, she's already dressed and raring to help Joan. I'm feeling a little queasy from the Lancashire Hot Pot and sleep in.

Father Bob is supposed to be at a parish meeting. So I don't think anything of it when the door opens.

"Mammie," I say, sitting up.

But it's Father Bob in his bathrobe. I grab a sweater from the chair to cover myself. Yet I don't know why. After all, he's my uncle. A priest. A man I've written letters to all my life. And I'm clothed. I have on a white cotton nightgown.

"Alice M'rie, I'm so sorry. I was dreaming . . . and stumbled into . . . I'm so sorry."

"Father Bob, it's okay. I thought you were at a meeting." But he makes no motion to leave.

"Father Bob, Mammie's expecting me downstairs. I've got to . . . ."

"Of course. Well then, Alice M'rie, I was looking at you in the church yesterday. What a fine woman you're turning out to be."

"Oh, thanks."

"Now, how about a hug?"

With that he comes toward me. He puts his arms around me, kisses me, and sticks his smelly cigarette tongue in my mouth. I can feel something hard through his old green dressing gown. I don't know what it could be, but it feels like a sin. I push him away hard as I can, and Father Bob crashes down on the bed.

"Alice M'rie, are ye all right?" Mammie calls up.

I can hear her step downstairs in the hall.

"Did ye fall out of bed?"

"Oh, I'm grand. A wasp came in the window. I swatted at it and tripped."

Mammie's up the stairs in a flash. Father Bob hides behind the drapes. I run to the window and began whooshing out the invisible wasp.

Mammie surveys the situation from the doorway.

"You should have seen him, Mammie. He was huge."

"Alice M'rie, ye made such a clunk. Ye've got to stop eating those sweeties."

Mammie goes to the window, looks out, and then starts to straighten up the bed.

I'm afraid to start a chat that might keep her in the room. All I want to do is wash out my mouth. I'm not sure if the smell of Sweet Afton that's lingering in the air belongs to me or Father Bob. I just hope Mammie doesn't smell it. I can see his slippers peeking out from the drapes.

Mammie smoothes the bed. "Alice M'rie, ye better start packing for London."

Mammie leaves, and Father Bob emerges from the drapes. He's pinned to the spot with embarrassment. And so we stand there.

I say, "I'll go into the loo and flush; the noise'll cover you leaving."

And I do. Father Bob leaves. I vomit. I cry. I brush my teeth till my gums bleed. I can't tell Mammie. It would hurt her.

True to his word, Father Bob takes us to London. We go down by train, lunch included: pork chops and silence. Father Bob and I are gagged with our secret. He starts reciting nursery rhymes.

To London
To London
To buy a fat pig.
Home again, home again
Jiggidy jig.

Then he laughs and lights up another fag.

It doesn't matter to me that our visit to London occurs not only on a foggy day, but a rainy one as well. It's nice to finally be there.

Father Bob waltzes us around Piccadilly Circus. "See, Alice M'rie, that's the statue of Eros up there."

Ha! Eros. Mammie hasn't a clue what he's referring to.

He must be terrified I'll tell. I can't tell. And he knows it. What can I say? O Mammie, I'm sorry, but Father Bob popped into the room this morning and stuck his tongue in my mouth. Committed a mortal sin, he did. And who will he go to Confession to? Huh? Well, he'll confess to himself, won't he? And he'll get himself off the hook, too (much as he did with that Indian lady), with those three Ave's, three Pater's, and three Glory Be's.

Atonement is a great thing. Father Bob plies me with Kit Kats, Cadbury Milk Trays, Black Magic, Turkish Delight, and Fry's Cremes. Little flags, stickers, purses, booklets, bookmarks. Any postcard I want. But the smell of him drives me crazy. I won't walk next to him at all. Not anymore. Never again. There he is, up front like a

Scout master, waving his brolly, with Mammie and me bringing up the rear. How could I have ever held hands with that big black blob! That beetle! That tub o' lard! That priest!

We're at St. Paul's Cathedral looking at the famous life-size portrait of Jesus knocking at the door. Gazing up at it, I imagine Jesus scolding me. He sounds just like Father Bob.

Well then, Alice M'rie, you held hands with a priest! Didn't you? Didn't you? And of your own free will, too. Missy, you committed a sin. You let your uncle, a priest, my right-hand man, hold your *haaaaaand*. You let him hold your hand. You lured him on, girl. All your foolish thoughts of romance. Your visions. Some enchanted evening you will see a stranger. You will see a stranger across a crowded room. Well, wishes come true.

No, no, Jesus. I didn't. I didn't lure. I don't know how to. 'Tis he's the priest. 'Tis he's the adult. I'm the child. Even with my romantic notions.

Mammie's confused. "Alice M'rie, what're ye staring at that picture for?"

"I dunno."

"And what's happened with ye and Bob? He says ye don't like him anymore."

"That was midsummer madness, Lord Dudley." And Mammie laughs at a line from *Auntie Mame*, a play Miss D. just revived at City Center.

We walk the streets in single file, Father Bob up ahead with his patent-leather hair, omnipresent fags, and nicotine-stained fingers. His clerical collar, fat knees, and phony Englishese. How I hate him and his Cheerio! *Cheerio*, then! Ta! Luv! I say! How 'bout a fag? Give us a kiss.

And his table manners. His slicing off the top of a soft-boiled egg with a one-two hit of the knife. His lining up the peas on the tongs of his fork-one, two, three, four, five—then smashing them with a wad o' spuds, a hit o' gravy, and cramming them all in his mouth at the same time. The same mouth that transforms bread and wine into Christ's body and blood.

Father Bob's whistling, "London Bridge is falling down, falling down, falling down. London Bridge is falling down, my fair lady."

Mammie and I are trailing behind. The rain is dousing us. Up the Mall. There's the palace. Down Knightsbridge, wave to Harrods. On to the British Museum, which not only has lost its charm, but will take too long to see. Then the fool forgets his bowler in the Trafalger Square loo. O the Holy Father must take off his hat to pee? Men are fools, they are. Old fools. All of them.

Pretending everything's hunky-dory, Father Bob scampers up Piccadilly. The rain is beating down on his head. His dripping hair is hanging there, framing his face, like two dead crows. Mammie is laughing. Father Bob says, "I say, Alice, it's not funny. That hat cost me fifty quid." *Quid.* Another of his Englishese expressions. He looks like an undertaker. Later on Mammie and I go to Harrods' ladies' room and bust our guts laughing at him. The fat old fool.

I've dropped the "Father." No more Father Bob for me. Just plain Bob. It kills Mammie.

We take a peek at the Tower and the Abbey. But these don't interest Bob. He's all fluffed up about taking us to Madame Tussaud's. The fog's lifted. It's now the hottest day London's seen since the night of the Big Fire.

Bob whisks us past the wax works of the royal family and Churchill. Down, down, down we go to the Chamber of Horrors. It's the Chamber of Horrors that thrills Bob. That's why we're here. It's dark, creepy, humid, and smells like horse sweat. Bob's pointing out the finer points of execution.

"There's the guillotine. The rack. The stew pot. Alice M'rie, it's a terrible thing, the harm people inflict on each other."

Is this an apology? Is this Bob's confession to me?

Madame Tussaud provides the tableaux vivants with appropriate blood-red lighting and a soundtrack of cries and whimpers for hanging, boiling, flaying, burning, each method more tortuous than the next.

Mammie's giggling. *Giggling.* My God, maybe she was Roman in a prior life. There's blood all over the place. Kids are screaming. And I collapse. Right there on the

floor of Madame Tussaud's. It's too hot. There's no ventilation. And I'm wondering whether Bob and I committed
a sin of impurity together. I haven't yet figured out if my
half is mortal or venial. If it's mortal, I'll burn in hell. If it's
venial, I'll sweat in purgatory. I don't know about Bob's
punishment.

We get me up. We get me out. We walk to
Westminster Cathedral, the Catholic one. And we sit in
the coolness known only to churches in summer.

This isn't the London Homer had in mind. But it
is London, not Ireland. And I was there. I loved what I
saw. Then we go back to Liverpool, where the other shoe
drops.

Bob says he wants to accompany "the ladies" back
to Ireland. Mammie's all smiles, thrilled to be having
more time with him.

"O Bob, what'll your parishioners do without
you?" *Do?* They'll be ecstatic not to see those stubby yel-
lowed fingers waving the Eucharist around. I'm disgusted.

Back again in Carrigeen, the Slatterys are in shock.

"Father Bob, Father Bob, why have ye come back?"

"I want to do something nice for Alice M'rie."

Bob doesn't say just what he wants to do, and ten-
sions are high. I won't sit by him at table, nor next to him
in the car.

"The marriage is off," says Dave.

And they all laugh. I get sick on Sunday and
won't go to his or any other Mass. Feck that special

indulgence. I've enough special indulgences from Bob to last a lifetime. I stay in bed looking at the Paps. I'm trying to read *Long Day's Journey into Night*, for Jed said there'd be a moment when I'd feel the need to read Irish family drama.

Bang! goes the kettle. Sweet Afton mingling with Players wafts up the stairs. It's a beautiful day and I don't care. I want to be back in New York on Lexington Avenue where I feel at home. I wonder what Jed's doing. It's Sunday. He's doing nothing. But Miss D . . . Ah, Miss D. She's having lunch on the terrace in the country. The General is mixing drinks at the bar, under that umbrella of his proclaiming *Ginder Ale.* Yet I'm in the country, too. Ireland is all "country." I hang out the window and think of my poor, sweet little Mitzi, hanging out her window in Astoria, hoping to maim this year's crop of caterpillars.

There's the road. There's the cows. There's D.D. down by the stream with them. The cows shite all over the grass. Yet they say from the sky, Ireland is so green. Like Oz. The tourist board says there are a hundred shades of green here, hundreds of interwoven patch-work pieces of green laced through with cow shite that you can't see from the sky. But it's there. I walk in it. It's not pretty. Blackberry bushes line the lane and prick my fingers when I go for the juice. Ireland on a Sunday. The day of rest. But not here. Not on a farm. And there's no rest ever in Carrigeen. Maybe if I wheedle a bit, they'll drive me into Killarney so I can see Haulie. No, I don't want to see any man.

I hear Dave's booted foot on the stair.

"Alice Maria . . ."

That's how he says it. Maria. Maria. They call the wind Maria.

"Yer uncle wants to propose something."

I like Dave. He hasn't a clue. I go down. Bob's standing in the kitchen under the picture of the Sacred Heart, nursing a short Paddy. And Mammie's sitting by the fire, looking quite bleak.

"Alice M'rie," says Bob, "you've not yet visited your father's ancestral home."

"No. Would I want to, though? Mammie, do you want to?" She says nothing. Pours herself another cup of tea.

"I never thought about it."

"It would complete the family picture for you. That's why I came back with you and your mother. To bring you up to your father's home. It's the least I can do."

"Mammie, what do you think?"

"I want nothing to do with it." She goes out to the haggard and stares at the cows.

I give a scad eye to Jesus. His hands are touching the edges of his bloody wound, while here in this kitchen another wound has opened up.

Bob, you traitor, you. You know Mammie doesn't want to visit Carey's old home up there on the mountain.

It's Tuesday. Mammie and I are returning to New York on Friday. Bob insists we go up to Coomacullin to see the house where Carey was born.

Dave suggests we hire a taxi driver from town. But Bob's adamant. He wants to drive us himself. All I want is to get it over with. I want to get back to New York to glamour. Pissing into a basin for two months is enough to make a girl weary.

Early Wednesday morning we get in the car. Bob asks Mammie which way we should go. Mind you, we forgot the map.

"Over there, on the other side of that," she says, pointing a gloved finger to the Paps. Then Bob takes off at his steady thirty miles per hour. Mammie is in front. I'm in back. On the seat next to me is an iced raisin Barmbrack loaf for tea, and a bottle of Paddy. Offerings for Carey's brother's widow and her daughter, who I guess is my cousin.

"Mammie, what're their names?"

"Kathleen's the one, I think. I'm not sure of the other."

Mammie's all decked out in her tipsy soufflé hat. I'm in my blazer with the crest signifying nothing. We head toward Killarney so Bob can buy a regional map. He comes back to the car with a map and a booklet for me entitled *A Souvenir of Killarney*. On the title page is a quote from Edmund Spenser.

"I say, Alice M'rie, has Mr. Harris introduced you to the great Spenser?"

"Mammie and I saw him in *Father of the Bride*."

Silence descends. We chug out of Killarney and proceed east on the Macroom road. There's nothing left to say. Bob and I have not a drop of palaver left.

The landscape changes from pastoral to rocky. We drive into the hills on what looks like an old laneway that's been roughly paved over. Fallen boulders form a gauntlet. The car windows are getting dusty. This is not the Irish landscape sought out by tourists. We drive on until the road dead-ends on a muddy goat's path, which goes straight up a mountain.

"Alice, are we heading the right way?" says Bob.

"I don't know at all."

"But Mammie, did you never go visiting when you were courting?"

Wrong thing to say. Cheeky little git.

"I've never been up there," says Mammie.

Bob consults his regional map. Through Headford PO, past Morley's Bridge, past Glenflesk church, onto Clonkeen. Then up. Up where? We get out of the car. Bob walks away to "relieve" himself. Mammie and I look up the hill. But it isn't a hill. It's a mountain. A huge, rocky, dusty mountain with nary a bit of green to dress it up.

Bob returns.

"I say, Alice, do you have to visit Mrs. Murphy? Better here than there."

My mammie pee on a rock? She'd rather die. Me too. And I have to go. All that fecking tea. Too much tea. Ireland is one mad tea party. We get back in the car.

"From the look of the map, this is it," Bob says.

Mammie is silent.

Bob starts the car again. Mammie takes off her gloves, puts them on, then takes them off again. I look at myself in the car mirror. My face is oily. My eyes are puffy. My bun is so squeezed on my head, I look bald. We're at a priest's mercy.

"Oh dear," says Bob, grabbing the gearshift and jerking it around. The car doesn't budge.

"Now, Bob . . ." says Mammie, and she puts her gloved hand on his black-suited arm. The gears domino, one, two, three, four, and we assault the hill. The cake's flung on the floor. The icing cracks.

"Jesus, Mary, and sweet St. Joseph!" hoots Bob as the car jerks forward, rolls back, and stalls again.

Mammie's face is shiny, moist, and red. She takes out her compact for a quick touch-up. Bob drags on his Afton. He wipes his brow with a large linen handkerchief with the initials *Rev. RS* embroidered in red in the corner. This perks him up.

"I say, Alice . . . damn hard. We didn't have hills like this in the Punjab. . . . Shall we have another go at it?"

The wheels are sinking in cow shite and mud. The air is sharp. There's nary a green leaf in sight. Bob eases his foot off of the brake and whisks into fourth gear. The car spins around. The bottle of Paddy smashes against the door.

Stink of whiskey. Broken glass. I jump out of the car. Mammie, too. Bob eases out of his side.

"These hills . . . eh, Alice M'rie."

"We could've gotten killed!" I scream. "Mammie, the fool can't drive." I give her a look I regret to this day. A look that indicated that she was she and I was I. We were no longer a "we."

"Alice M'rie, apologize to Father Bob."

"I will not. We should've gotten a taxi, if ye're so intent on me seeing Carey's old home."

"Now, Alice"—he drops the "Marie"—"what do you want us do? We don't want to ruin your holiday."

They both stand there gazing at me, as if I have the answer. I walk away. It's all so bleak. Sheep come and go. There isn't a house to be seen. We're all dolled up with no place to go. I begin to cry.

"I just want to go back to New York."

Bob hands Mammie his handkerchief. From her handbag she takes out her tube of Elizabeth Arden's "Stop Red" and daubs it on her lips. Mammie's silent. I hope I don't have to pay for my truth. She hands me Bob's handkerchief.

"Wipe yer face, Alice M'rie."

Our sweat commingles.

I look up at the mountain.

"Is that where he's from?"

I don't say his name: Daddy. Or Father. Or Carey. Neither do they.

"It is a long way up, and the cake and whiskey are ruined," says Bob.

"Yes," says Mammie. "We wouldn't want to try again and damage Bob's rented car."

Silence. Bob starts the car and we drive back to Killarney, leaving the broken cake and glass on the mountain.

ON OUR LAST DAY IN CARRIGEEN, we plan to stay up all night. Dave says this custom originated during the Famine, when those who were going to remain home would hold a wake of sorts in the West Room for the departing emigrant. Everyone stayed up till dawn. Then they sang the emigrant down the road on his way to America, never to return. Never to be seen again. But that's not us. Mammie vows we'll return next year. And the next. And the next one after that.

Bob has slipped away, back to Liverpool, at the crack of dawn. Mammie said it'd break his heart to see us leave before him. Oh, the relief. It's as if a great black stone had been lifted from my head. I'm even standing straighter.

Mammie and I take the bus to Killarney for a last look around. We're going to buy a leg of lamb. Mammie's going to cook it, just the way she cooks it for Miss D. A pound of Nescafé for Irish coffee. And a pint of double cream for the whipped topping. I buy my last lot of Cadbury's chocolate bars. And the English papers.

Mammie buys Dave a bottle of Paddy, Mary Falvey a bottle of Yardley cologne, the lads winter cardigans. Farewell offerings.

We visit the old haunts. The lanes. The cobbler. The butcher. Scott's Hotel. The Sullivans. Haulie gives me a pretty gold wool Aran sweater. Gold, mind, not your ordinary white. We promise to write. He gives me a tentative hug.

"Ye're the real article," he verifies.

There are tears in my eyes. Then Mammie and I light a candle at the friary to ensure that the *Mauretania* won't sink.

In the evening, Dave brings down the Victrola and we play *My Fair Lady*. D.D. makes Irish coffee. Mary Falvey, grinning wildly, settles back in front of the fire, announcing, "Ah, the whish-key t'roo d'wipped cream is killin' me."

Mammie takes over the kitchen. I take a walk round the haggard and out to the apple orchard. Part of me, a little, teeny, tiny bit, is sad I didn't appreciate *Home* as much as Mammie hoped I would. My saying "I just want to go back to New York" up there in Coomacullin killed her. I know it did.

Mary Falvey has set the table in the West Room with the good china. I'm sitting under the picture of the three blind girls. There's Guinness all round. And Paddy and Dubonnet. And for me, a Coca-Cola. A real treat. The skin of the roast lamb crackles. Mammie has made an *au jus déglace*. None of yer doughy gravy here. Yellow turnips, or Swedes, as Dave calls them, sport a glazing of brown sugar.

And the spuds, newly plucked from the ground, lie on a blue platter slathered with sweet butter. Dave proclaims, "Ye'll never ate d'likes o'dese in New York, Alice Maria." And he's right. The cream cake, with blackberries I picked up the lane, is as light as a feather. And through the haze of Sweet Afton and Irish coffee, order had been restored.

Mammie and I eye our pictures on the sideboard, and Mary Falvey begins to cry. "O Alice, please God, ye'll come Home again soon."

Dave cranks up the Victrola and puts on *Peter Pan*.

My child, my very own
Don't be afraid, you're not alone.

I'm up in the bedroom looking out at the Paps. It's around midnight, at the end of a lingering Celtic twilight in the west of Ireland, at the dawn of the sixties. Downstairs I can hear Mammie singing something.

We'll build a dear little nest
Somewhere out in the West
And let the rest of the world go by.

I feel woopsie. I can't use the po. I've got to go outside. And I do. In the apple orchard under a full August moon I vomit. And I cry. My summer vacation's over. I grew up.

And evening full of
the linnet's wings

ON OUR WAY BACK from the Skelligs, we stop at St. James the Apostle, Church of Ireland, in a nearby village.

"This is as pretty a church as where Fred Astaire marries Audrey Hepburn at the end of *Funny Face*," I tell La Greca. And it is. Reached by an old stone bridge, St. James sits at the mouth of a winding stream feeding into Dunmanus Bay. In *St. James: A Parish History*, published in 1992 for the church's two hundredth anniversary, an old historian described the view from the churchyard we saw that evening:

> *To see a sunset on that harbour of a summer's evening would cast a ray of light upon one's bosom and that would make it look like a pathway to heaven.*

We start poking around the old cemetery, reading aloud eighteenth-century headstones. Many Shannons are buried here. Geoffrey is trying, to no avail, to find the graves of the young Shannon boys who once lived and died in our Big House, when who should suddenly appear through the stile but Sally Johnston.

"Sally," I say, "you must meet David La Greca. He's heard all about you."

"Sure, girl, why would he even hear about me?"

"Because you're fabulous," I say. And Sally laughs, *fabulous* not being a word in her vernacular.

"I'm here to have a look at my grave," says Sally. "I'm going right there." And she points to an empty grassy plot by the walk leading to the church's front door. "I'll miss nothing there, girl, nothing at all. They'll all have to pass by me to get in." As we continue reading headstones, we see Sally picking errant weeds from her plot.

Later that evening, chicken in the AGA and wine in hand, La Greca, Geoffrey, and I walk our old laneway. La Greca can't get over Sally.

"She is fabulous. She could lecture a theology class with the spiritual connection she's made between being alive and being dead. Some of the guys we've seen die from AIDS went peacefully," says La Greca. "They just crossed over that bridge."

"Peter Pan says, 'Death must be an awfully big adventure,' as he's about to walk the plank," I offer.

"Are you saying they made the same connection?" asks Geoffrey.

"Maybe," says La Greca.

"They cut that line from the musical," I add.

The theology discussion fizzles. We've had too much wine. And the early evening air is intoxicating. Last rays of sunlight dance on the fern-lined walk of mossy rocks and foxgloves pushing up from the ground, getting ready for next spring's flower show. My eyes catch something moving. I look. It disappears. Is it a fairy? Maybe the spirits of the laneway are playing peekaboo with us. In true fairyland fashion, all is not what it seems. It's night. Yet the sun remains high. There's a scent of jasmine in the air. Yet there is no jasmine.

La Greca wants a last poke around the Big House. I tell him about the West Room and how in the old days, every house had this designated room facing toward fairyland.

"Alice believes in fairies," says Geoffrey. And La Greca smiles, his eyes glancing westward.

We fall silent as we stand outside the old front door, with its rusted brass knob and its glass transom that has illuminated every person who ever entered this house. As the magical day draws to a close, I think of Jed Harris and his promise of happiness in the guise of a musical about a fairy.

TRUE TO HIS WORD, two house seats have arrived at Miss D.'s by messenger for the New Year's Day matinee of *Peter Pan*.

Miss D. says house seats are reserved for important people with clout. That's Mammie and me. We're practically onstage; so close I can read the *Daily News* racing sheet along with the trombone player. In my pocket is a fistful of dimes scooped up from Jed's bed. He has commanded me to call at intermission with a critique. He also gave me a few dollars for a program. Not just a *Playbill*, mind, but a souvenir program.

I can hardly breathe with excitement. My hands are sweating through my gloves. Mammie says ladies always wear gloves at the theater. I look at my program. Everyone else is doing the same thing, except they're not wearing gloves.

Lights down, curtain up. We're in a nursery with a huge French window. *Whoosh!* The window opens wide. It's Peter Pan. It's Mary Martin. She's flying. I don't even see the wires. The audience goes wild.

"First I'll blow the fairy dust on you!"

We're so near, a little gold fairy dust shimmers down onto Mammie and me. Mine's on my glove. I try to keep my hands still so I won't lose it. Then Peter teaches the children to fly. He wants them to think wonderful thoughts. And they scream out, *Christmas! Flowers! Candy!*

I think: Mitzi, Homer, Jed, tea 'n' cakes, Babka, Central Park in the rain. Maybe Mammie's thinking wonderful thoughts as well. Maybe she's hoping that the two of us will fly away to somewhere else. Beyond Astoria. Beyond Lexington Avenue.

. . . and straight on till morning.

The Hershey bar I'm clutching melts in my hand. Jed would love this show.

Intermission.

I run up the aisle to call Jed.

"O Jed, it's beautiful. It's the best show on Broadway. It'll win an Oscar."

Wheeze, drag, pause.

"Darling, tell me about Mary."

"O Jed, she's wonderful. She flies so well. She has such sturdy legs."

Drag, puff, drag.

"And she's not too long in the tooth for the part?"

"Jed! She looks about twelve."

The line behind me is fuming. But I'm on the phone with Jed Harris. *The* Jed Harris. Don't they know who he is? *Jed, Jed, Jed.* I keep saying his name. I want them to hear it. I'm not simply calling Forest Hills to check on the baby-sitter like they are. I'm calling Jed Harris, who invented Broadway! *The* Jed Harris, who got me and my mammie house seats for the greatest musical ever written. With that, my dimes run out, the line breathes a sigh of relief, and I return to my seat.

Tinker Bell is dying in a jar, and Mary is beseeching the audience to clap their hands if they believe in fairies. Of course we do. Homer's a fairy. And John and David and Michael, too. Mammie and I love fairies. We applaud and applaud and scream out, "We do believe in fairies. We do believe. We do." I'm half out of my seat with excitement when Mammie pulls me back down.

Then it's over. It's all over so quickly. The lights go up and everyone starts to stream out. Mammie and I stay in our seats. We can't budge.

"Can we stay and see it again," I ask, "like a movie?"

We're the last to leave. We stand in the back of the theater and look at the Winter Garden stage. Mammie says they'll do it again tonight. Homer told me Mary takes a long nap between shows, sips herbal tea, and practices yoga. We buy the album in the lobby. Jed must have slipped Mammie a few bucks, too.

As we head for the subway, it starts to snow. Mammie puts the album under her coat to keep it dry. I run the show in my head, and run the show in my head, and run the show in my head. I want to remember it forever. We've seen a real Broadway show, my mammie and me. On the Broadway my Jed created.

La Greca breaks into my reverie. "Guys, I figured out what you should name the stables—'Faileth Not.' I saw the phrase on one of the old tombstones today, near Sally Johnston's. It just read *Faileth Not*. It's what you and this place are all about."

i will arise and go now

BY THE TIME LA GRECA LEFT, Geoffrey and I were near the end of our first stay in the stables. Every day we vacuumed, and every day the dirt returned. We were still sleeping on the floor. I was still walking with a stoop. And we hadn't made love. To rescue our so-called vacation, we drove up to Cork City to spend a night in a hotel. But when we got there, after taking a hot shower that seemed to last a year, all we had the energy to do was lie in bed and rub each other's iron-stiff necks.

Nine days before we were to return to New York, I heard a noise. I heard it in the middle of the night. From behind the hermitage came a faint meow. It woke me up. Geoffrey heard it in the morning as he put on the kettle. I didn't tell him. Nor he me. What would we do with a cat in Ireland? Sirrah, a cat in Ireland is a consummation devoutly to be wished. Yet with Ireland's stringent rabies quarantine law, a cat of ours here would be in for a lonely life indeed. Pets may leave Ireland for, say, America, but upon return they must suffer six months' incarceration in quarantine.

Meows persisted.

"Cat . . . ?" said I.

"Meow," said the cat.

Up popped a jet-black kitten with lettuce-green eyes. And in a twinkling of those eyes, we were hers.

We had but a week to tame her. Were it a month, we could easily fatten her up, but now we had to work fast. Out came the bowls of milk, tidbits of bacon, smidgens of chicken. Audrey said farm cats love bread soaked in milk. And so she did. Pretty soon the cat was in the house. On the couch. And on our bed.

"That's good luck f'r ye, girl," proclaimed Sally Johnston. "A black cat showing up out of the blue."

"Is it a gift from the fairies, Sally? That's what I want to know." And Sally Johnston looked away, so as not to offend the possibility.

The Johnstons swore they'd feed her when we left, since "the cat" (as we kept calling her) was considered good luck. Then we headed to Bantry to stock up on cat food with fanciful names like Rascal's Reward and Choosy for this young lady of property.

We couldn't keep calling her "the cat." Eventually we settled on Thomasina, after the young girl in Tom Stoppard's *Arcadia*, a play I loved and saw three times. Thomasina, a mathematical idiot savant, longs only to waltz with her tutor, who upon her tragic death winds up his days in a hermitage. And so the cat who turned up by our hermitage became our Thomasina.

That last day as we drove at dawn down the laneway, lit only by the morning star, a small black cat stood guard by the hermitage: Thomasina, our bright particular star. The AGA would keep the house warm. Thomasina would be fed, would have shelter, would not be wandering the roads. It was all we could do. We would not see her again until we returned for Christmas.

BACK IN NEW YORK, it dawned on us just how difficult it would be to live in Ireland *and* to also live in New York. The songwriter and performer Peter Allen always set Geoffrey and me laughing by saying he was "bicoastal." We knew he was putting a spin on "bisexual," but it was his ease in living on two coasts that captured our imaginations.

We'd imagine him in a Hawaiian shirt kicking up his heels in New York with the Rockettes, then stopping off in London to play the Palladium, and finally back home to Australia to cool his heels before he did it again. All this, mind, carrying only hand luggage and a toothbrush.

But after those nineteen days in Ireland in August, Geoffrey and I finally got a bead on just how skewed our vision of "an international lifestyle" was. You'd think we'd have understood the huge difference between going out to Fire Island every weekend and having to plan months ahead to fly to Ireland. But we hadn't. Then again, if we had really thought about how complicated it would be, we might never have bought a house across the Atlantic Ocean. Having an "international lifestyle" is a damned hard thing for mere mortals.

During the two years it took us to turn the stables into a livable cottage, we were thoroughly engaged. A stringent order of work had to be followed in order to accomplish the renovation. So whether we were in New York or Ireland, we were still "doing the stables." It was like running a small family business. We made lists, held decorating meetings, reviewed our financials. We read Irish decorating books, English decorating books. We looked at paint chips and obsessed about the choices. We carried around pictures of the stables and showed them to anyone who expressed the least bit of interest. We were so busy and distracted, we never had time to think about what actually living in Ireland would entail. We centered on accomplishing our goal—to live in the stables. And live there we did.

However, at the end of the day, stables are stables. They were just a project for us to cut our teeth on. The Big House, the house we had fallen in love with, loomed on the ridge. And we still hadn't a clue what to do with it.

But we had realized that to properly restore the Big House, and to beautifully decorate the stables, we would have to give up something. We could not maintain the fantasy of living in New York, Fire Island, and Ireland.

A decision of the heart and the pocketbook had to be made. We'd have to sell our house on Fire Island.

Back at Magic Flute in September, as I was trying to shift around the love in my heart, it was clear that selling the place would be hard. When neighbors greeted me on the boardwalk, I found I was already missing them, even the ones I never really liked. Islanders to whom I only gave a nod of the head became part of the tapestry I was going to have to sacrifice for a tapestry not yet woven. On clear autumn nights, Geoffrey and I would sit on the top deck, looking up at the stars and across the ocean.

"Ireland," I'd say, pointing.

"Spain," he'd say. "We're facing south."

"Ireland," I'd say.

We knew we had to drop a few hints about leaving. Yet my theater chum Maggie McCorkle threw herself against our gate when I mentioned it.

"You can't," she said. "You can't leave."

And there were tears in her eyes.

Nearly every day a new epiphany came.

Take decorating, for example. Every time we'd plonk down five bucks for a British shelter magazine, we'd ooh and aah about how beautiful everything looked in its glossy pages. But now we knew if we wanted the stables to be as beautiful as the places we saw in *Period Home* or *Country Living*, we'd have to figure out how to do it ourselves. And it would be neither easy nor cheap.

In the seventies, when I moved down the block into Geoffrey's apartment, all we did was merge his few sticks of furniture with mine to make a home. When we bought

Magic Flute, it came furnished, as is the custom with Fire Island houses. Over the years we had had time to poke around and buy cheap antiques. But furnishing and decorating in Ireland was going to be far more of a challenge.

When friends would ask if we were going to hire an interior decorator, I'd say no. Our old chum *New York Times* writer Albin Krebs used to call them "inferior desecrators." And we wanted none of that. We would do the job ourselves.

When Geoffrey and I returned to Cork for Christmas, we knew the tasks that awaited us. We just weren't prepared for the coldest winter in living memory. It was beautiful—every dawn was pink, every sunset fiery—but it was below freezing and hard to keep the house warm. The fields had turned a sage green and were crunchy underfoot. The pond was frozen. The moss compacted and turned crisp and fragile. This was an Ireland I had never seen before.

Our plan was to paint the interior of the stables. We'd brought over pigments to mix by hand. Since each room opens into the next one, the colors would have to flow seamlessly from one space to the next. The room nearest the Big House, which once housed the pony cart, we would paint a Creamsicle orange. The next room, our large living and cooking area, with the fireplace and AGA, would be the color of unsalted butter. The mudroom, with its boots, rain gear, tools, and washer/dryer, would be a salted-butter yellow. The bathroom, dominated by the huge Victorian tub, was to be a yellowy chartreuse to complement the apple-green sink. The last room on the western end, our bedroom—lilac.

But living in color was not in the cards for us that Christmas. The hard freeze that enveloped Ireland held the upper hand. Since the paint had to be mixed on-site, and since it did not have the preservatives of, say, a Benjamin Moore, it "seized." Buckets of it clotted, making it impossible for us to paint.

Other things happened as well. Thomasina almost died from a botched spaying. And on the bitterly cold, moonlit night of the Winter Solstice, a young, glamorous Frenchwoman named Sophie du Plantier was bludgeoned to death on the laneway of her holiday home, just a few villages away. As poet John Montague wrote in his article about Sophie for the *New Yorker*, "It was the first murder in these remote parts since Civil War days." When Geoffrey returned to New York after New Year's, I stayed on for a few weeks alone in the stables to nurse Thomasina. Sophie's murder scared the daylights out of me.

In March I returned to Ireland. It was spring, and Thomasina was well again. Joe O'Brien, a local painter, had filled our rooms with color, and they looked beautiful. The orange melted into the yellow, which melted into the chartreuse, which melted into the lilac. I'd go from room to room admiring the rainbow. As Kelly, my old Cherry Grove pal, used to say, "Life is meant to be lived in color."

Johnnie K., the builder, had made us a wonderful front and side terrace from large flagstones. I began to plant geraniums, pansies, rosemary, and thyme in what would become a border garden. Purple foxgloves and violets were up in the lane, and the air smelled sweet. The stables were beginning to look like a home. Because I wanted some hand in the painting, I decided to paint the Dutch door vermilion to welcome the fairies.

Thomasina and I walk the fields of an evening. It's our ritual, she and I. Without the beach to roam, I've begun to think of the waving grass as sand.

The light determines what time we take to the fields. It must shimmer with the expectation of night yet be reluctant to give up the day. The land is softening. There's a hint of gold in the grass. The buds of the hawthorn are plumping up. The temperature is a balmy fifty-five. I'm standing on the flagstone terrace looking west. Beyond Bantry Bay the mountains are greener with the coming of spring. Thomasina is waiting. She knows the drill. She's sitting on the kitchen table waiting for me to pull on my wellies.

Come on, then, girl. And my cat leaps from the table and gives herself a long, lithe stretch. Every evening we take a slightly different jaunt to end up at our favorite place, the field at the foot of the Ring Fort.

Thomasina bounds out the door, heading to the top of the stone stile to survey the daffodils. The courtyard is a swath of yellow. Old daffs, probably planted by the Shannons, have multiplied over the years. Their pale yellow bonnets, bobbing on their green necklaces, sway in the moist breeze.

Thomasina and I stand on a stone wall to survey a natural landscape that has taken hundreds of years to evolve. The ditches, the hedgerows, the laneway are bursting with primroses, bluebells, snowdrops, violets. I look over to my just painted vermilion door to inspect Nellie Moser, a pink and white clematis growing by leaps and bounds. But my pace is too slow for Thomasina, and she scoots ahead of me. Here in the fields, I'm aware of every step I take. Every step is a meditation on this ancient land.

We go down to the boundary between the Johnstons' land and ours to watch the cows walking a lazy conga line to the cow-crush, an iron cage filled with hay silage, their feed. This is our nightly entertainment.

Thomasina bounds across an ancient stone wall Geoffrey discovered while clearing brush. He burned back a ganglion of blackberry canes and ivy that had obscured the wall for years. Now it frames the pond. Nearby we found two buried walls that predate the stables. It's my hope they may be connected with a Ring Fort.

During the Bronze Age, circular settlements—called Ring Forts—were built on high ground in view of water so their occupants could see the enemy approach by either land or sea. Superstition has it that doom will come to one who disturbs a Ring Fort, for the rings are believed to be inhabited by fairies. But I'm not afraid. I am standing in the center of this sacred space with my cat, who very well may have been a housewarming gift from the fairies.

Suddenly Thomasina gets her hackles up. My little cat's heart must be beating proudly for alerting me to something I have never seen before: There on a far wall is a red fox.

Feeling blessed, for this meditation is the nearest I get to prayer, Thomasina and I leave the Ring Fort and head for our favorite spot, a large boulder poked up in the middle of a field. A few stars are out. All is still. It will rain in an hour or so. In the morning my daffodils will gleam. Thomasina and I sit.

The last song from *Abbey Road* pops into my head, and I start to sing.

> *Once there was a way to get back homeward.*
> *Once there was a way to get back home.*

This rock. These green fields. This cat. This house. This Ireland. Thomasina climbs on my lap. She seems to be purring in tune. Night is falling. It's hard to see. Then Thomasina and I go home, she to her milk and me to the fire.

for always night and day

SUMMER IS OVER and Mammie and I are back in Astoria. I'm sneezing. And the sneezing won't stop.

We're not in the door two minutes when Carey proclaims, "Ye're sneezing. Them foreigners on that boat gave ye the plague."

"*Ship*, D.," says Mammie, already banging chops in the frying pan.

"Kelly, the boy from Killan, is dead," says Carey.

"How'd he die?" asks Mammie.

And they're off. Nothing's changed but me, my sin and my incessant sneezing. It's a sad thing to be starting eighth grade, Kleenex in one hand, heavy heart in the other. I'm driving Mammie and Carey crazy. Even old Mitzi is snarling. I thought she'd have pined away and died for the sight of me.

Mammie and I aren't saying much to each other. Going Home knocked us out. The truth is, Mammie and I have less to banter about. Father Bob is wedged between us.

"O Alice M'rie, ye're not writing to Father Bob and ye're not writing in your diary either."

I'm not. What can I say? Tell her the truth? Break her heart?

Anyway, the pressure's on. I've got to get into a good Catholic high school. Emphasis on *good*.

"O Alice M'rie," coos Mammie, "Marymount's the place for ye. Ye could walk down to Miss D.'s after school. I can just see ye as a Marymount girl."

But Marymount doesn't want me. I didn't score well on their multiple-choice test. There wasn't a single essay question, only acbdaadba. Choose one. Choice isn't up my alley. I don't give a feck. Rich girls go to Marymount. Rich girls with pageboy hairdos. But oh, the silences after I fail. Even Homer's sad. He knows Mammie wanted to put a feather in her cap called Marymount, and I dashed it to the ground.

Worse, no school wants me. Not even Blessed Sacrament, where all they do is teach you to type. I don't want to learn to type. Mammie is heartbroken.

"O Alice M'rie, I t'ought ye'd do better with all yer talk, all yer books. What can I tell them at Home?"

Carey doesn't give a damn that I failed. He's thrilled to have a new drum to bang. He's crowing about how I should stay home and keep the house clean. Then Mammie says the law says I must go to high school. And Carey crows even louder.

"Send her down to LICE. That's what she deserves—LICE."

Long Island City High, with boys, guns, and dope. It'll be Jailhouse Rock.

215

By Easter, every girl in my class but me has gotten into a *good* Catholic high school. You'd think they never owned a good dress, the way they go on about the uniforms.

"My uniform is the cutest," says poxy-faced Joanie Sheehan, thrilled to pieces to be going to *the* Mary Louis Academy in Jamaica, Queens. "It's maroon."

Feck! And pudgy little Annie McHugh, embarking on her sucking-up-to-the-nuns path at Holy Cross. "I'm in plaid. Green plaid," she says.

Plaid! I've worn plaid all my life. I want taffeta.

With no prospects but LICE, which will take anybody, Mammie and I pay a visit to our parish priest, old Father Lyons. We practically go down on our knees with the begging. After a lot of "Oh, she's a good girl. We're praying she has a vocation, and of course, we'll contribute to the building fund," Father Lyons writes a note to the Mother Superior of St. Michael's Academy in Manhattan. And I'm in. I'm in disgrace.

Another long summer looms, but this year without a visit to Ireland. I'm bigger. My hair's thinner, browner, and not so red. Everything I do is infused with the constant gnaw of failure. Some of the girls in my class are going to camp, or working. Working and getting paid! That's what Veronica Perelli is doing in her father's right-by-Carnegie-Hall flower store.

"Oh," says she, "I see the stars."

Nothing so grand is in the works for me. I'm going into the city to help Mammie help Miss D. And I'm

216

going to read *The Great Gatsby*, *Plutarch's Lives*, *A Tree Grows in Brooklyn*, and *Green Mansions*.

Father Bob sent me a graduation card of a Scottie wearing a big red bow and holding a diploma in his mouth. Homer gave me a little leather box from Georg Jensen containing a silver oak-leaf pin.

"The mighty oak was sacred to the Romans," he says, pinning the pin to my uniform pocket. "It's the strongest tree, the last to lose its leaves. That's you, m'dear."

On my last day of eighth grade, Reverend Mother summons me in. She's feathering her novitiate nest.

"Alice," she says, "God is calling you. That's why you didn't get into the high school you wanted. Because God wants you for himself."

Ah, no. Not this. I don't want to lock horns with a woman who looks like she's growing one. God isn't calling me. He wants nothing to do with me. I concentrate on a bowl of sour balls on the Reverend Mother's desk.

Reverend Mother shines her glasses and replaces her hands under her wimple.

"Your mother's worked hard all her life so you could have a proper education. Isn't it time you did something for her? Would you like a sour ball whilst pondering God's call?"

Reverend Mother proffers me the bowl with her right hand, the hand with her gold wedding ring that proves she's married to Christ. Boy, he must be blind. I take a lime one.

"Ah, green. Your love of Ireland extends even to sour balls."

We sit in silence, except for me crunching on the sour ball.

"Now, I shan't keep you. I know you must go into the city to help out your mother. That is why I want you to consider . . ."

I'm sweating bullets. I nearly choke on the sour ball.

"ReverendMotherIdon'tbelieveGodscallingmeand Idontwanttobeanun."

Reverend Mother lets out a breath that nearly blows me down. Then she gets up and shows me to the door. I'm scared she'll give me a clap on the head.

"Pity, turning your back on God like that . . . tch-tch-tch. . . . You know, Alice, you'll never have a day's luck."

I don't tell Mammie about this.

I hate St. Michael's. The déclassé-ness of it all. Girls in groups bound together by their love of Tab, Rock, Elvis, Sandra, Annette, and Ann-Margret. St. Michael's girls bound together by navy blue jumpers and beanies, walking arm in arm through the underground subway passage that connects Sixth Avenue to Eighth Avenue. St. Michael's girls headed to the outdoor bathroom that freezes in winter. Toilets overflowing with menstrual blood, shite, and sanitary napkins. The nuns say we must offer it up.

I'm learning nothing, and I don't want to learn anything. I learn more from Jed on a Saturday than I learn here in a month. ReligionFrenchEnglishAmericanHistoryMath.

218

And Gym. Take my clothes off in a room filled with girls wearing Maidenform bras? No, I won't.

The lunchroom smell is getting me down, too. I can't abide these girls eating their smelly bologna-tunaheadcheeseVelveetahamandSwisscheese sandwiches. With soda. Soda and dusty cookies sold by Sister Mikey (as they call her) for the volleyball team. Mammie makes me a thermos of hot chocolate and butter-and-sugar sandwiches on white Pepperidge Farm bread. That's my lunch.

I spare Mammie how terrible it is. I keep seeing her groveling to Father Lyons, saying we're related to Nanno Nagle.

"Oh, Alice M'rie would be thrilled to go to St. Michael's with the Irish Presentation Sisters. We're related to Nanno—the woman who founded the order, y'know."

One day my schoolbag falls. The thermos breaks. Hot chocolate is spilled all over the floor. Sister Pius swoops down.

"Miss Carey, is that yours?" She knows damn well it is.

"Why do you bring provisions from home, when we sell soda and cookies to help *your* volleyball team?"

Silence. How can I say anything with Pam 'n' Terry 'n' Sandy 'n' Linda all agog to hear my brogue. I want to say, I don't give a feck for soda or volleyball, you silly old bitch. But I'm silent. I get a demerit for insubordination.

I'm mopping up the floor with the janitor's mop. The girls are laughing. Barbara Villenova, she of the hairy

219

legs, says, "Allie, we'll help you talk like us. When we're t'roo wit' you"—ha ha ha—"Sister'll think you're from d' Bronx."

I mop. I leave. I run out the back door by the toilets and cut out. I run down Thirty-fourth Street. Take down my bun and let my hair flow like Alice in Wonderland. Mammie likes my mean little bun. She says I look refined. I don't want to merely look refined, I want to look English. I'm sick of looking Irish. And I want to sound like James Mason.

With the dollar a day I get from Mammie, who thinks I spend it on sweets, I cut school when I can and go to the movies. I want to see every English movie ever made so I can learn to speak like a thin-skinned-long-boned-pale-cigarette-smoking-gin-drinking-dog-loving English person. Everyone thinks the English are smart because they have English accents. Everyone thinks me quaint because I have an Irish brogue.

Well, so will I. I see every picture I can starring James Mason. His voice will be my voice. He has a mumble that's ever so attractive. I'm even pitching my voice lower to sound just like him. Then I show up at Miss D.'s at three-thirty, and Mammie and I have our tuna and tea with Homer.

"Little Alice," says Homer, "you need some sprucing up. Big Alice, a few grown-up outfits would—"

Mammie bristles at the word "grown-up." So Homer shuts up. I'm uncomfortable. Just a bit, mind. Homer and I have a secret between us. He saw me on Fifty-seventh Street coming out of the Sutton Theater.

Gave me a wink, then got into a cab. I winked back. Conspirators, that's what we are.

I'm getting older by the day. Pretty soon I'll never have to eat tuna fish again. I glance down at my white shins with their soft coating of grown-up hair. I hate it. As the cup comes to my mouth, I can't avoid touching the pimple next to my lip with my hand. It's all that hot chocolate and sugar.

Homer tries again. "Ladies, I was up at Susan's just as she was cleaning out her closet. 'Susie,' I said, 'Little Alice, Big Alice's girl, is just about your size,' and without hesitating she said, 'Homer, I don't want these dresses anymore.'"

Susan Strasberg is a beauty. That's because she's Jewish. It's the Mediterranean influence. Olive oil. Rosemary. Wine. Exotic nose and eyes. She's a friend of Miss D.'s. And she's pals with Marilyn Monroe. Once I saw the two of them through Miss D.'s kitchen porthole. It was when Susan was on Broadway in *Picnic*. No pimples on her face. Profiles, hair, smiles, and teeth—Marilyn and Susan.

Homer goes upstairs and comes down with a Bergdorf shopping bag spilling over with grown-up dresses.

"Susie had these made up when she was in *Time Remembered*. Now, look at that!"

Homer holds a dress up in front of me and starts to sing, "A pretty girl is like a melody . . ."

221

Soon I have five Susan Strasberg grown-up-pretty dresses. No cotton-starchy Mother Mary blue stuff here, but velvet and linen, ribbons and belts.

"Girl, take down that hair. Big Alice, she could be a Breck girl." And Homer reaches over and takes out the hairpins that pinch and scold my head. I feel pretty. I can see Mammie bristle.

I'm a new me, and it's brilliant. I've taken three of Susan's dresses to St. Michael's (cleverly hidden in shopping bags) and stashed them in my locker. Now when I cut out of school in the afternoon, I take one of the dresses to the ladies' room in a nice hotel, where I change in a stall from uniform to dress. Then I take my hair down, put my uniform in a purple Bergdorf shopping bag, and walk to the Waldorf, where I sit in a big wing chair for an hour or so reading *Cue* magazine, looking at my schoolbooks, or writing in my diary. Then I go to the ladies', change back into my uniform, and go down to Miss D.'s to help Mammie out.

Stealth, silence, cunning, and Susan Strasberg's dresses get me through the winter. Then one day, out of the blue, winds of change began to howl around 110 East Fifty-fifth Street. And Astoria, too. As I trot into Doubleday's bookstore, I bump into Homer trotting out.

"Dwa-ling, what are you doing here?" My goose starts cooking.

"Homer, dah-ling! Why, fancy meeting you here."

222

"Is this a saint's day? Some obscure saint, like lovely Dymphna, patron of naughty girls? Is that why Sister gave you a half day?"

"Dymphna is the saint of the mentally disturbed."

"Dwa-ling, you look so pretty in Susie's dress, I'll blow you to a hamburger."

Homer and I head for Hamburger Heaven, where old black men in waiter-white strap customers into little high chairs with attached trays.

"When I'm blue, I head right to here," says Homer. "I told Miss D. to abandon '21' and come here, where they'll treat her just like a child."

"Just think," I say, "she's eating lunch down the street." In choreographic glee we point toward "21." "And who's happier?"

"We are," says Homer.

Awkwardness creeps in. I know Homer knows that Mammie doesn't know about my secret double life. He begins to sing in my ear.

"A secret, a secret. I know she has a secret."

"Homer, people are looking at us."

"As well they should, dwa-ling. As well they should."

My mind is whirling. Should I confess? No, *confide*. Confide, that's it. Homer is my one true friend. He won't hurt me, or yell at me.

Sam, one of the older waiters, comes over.

"Why, Mr. Poupart, you should be on Broadway. Now, how 'bout a nice slice of cake for the young lady?"

"Oh, Sam, you're sweet," says Homer, quoting Marilyn Monroe in *Gentlemen Prefer Blondes*.

In silence, I delve into my devil's food cake.

"Dwa-ling, will you please tell your fairy god-mother why you're walking the streets when you should be in school?"

I smile and say nothing. Homer pays the check and we stroll up Madison Avenue.

Alice, you ninny, he's cracked the door. You'd better say something.

"Homer . . . I don't like St. Michael's. The girls laugh at me. They say I'm different."

"And you are, dwa-ling."

"Some even say I'm strange."

"I wouldn't go as far as to say that."

"I'm not strange. I'm just like you."

"Big Alice wonders what happened to your voice."

"I want to sound like James Mason."

"Dwa-ling, please tell her you want to sound like Vivien Leigh."

"Don't tell that I cut school, okay? I'll tell Mammie eventually."

Homer puts his arm around me, and we walk uptown in silence.

BY JUNE THE JIG IS UP. I have succeeded, in that I have failed everything but Religion and English. St. Michael says I must get out or go to summer school.

Mammie and I are sitting in Miss D.'s kitchen with my report card. Mammie's crying.

"Alice M'rie, what'll we do? I'll have to send ye back to Ireland. Maybe ye could help out Mary Falvey. My heart's broken. I can't tell Carey. Who can I tell? I'm so embarrassed. There's no one I can tell."

Homer trots down the kitchen stairs.

"Dwa-lings, flash, flash! This house is sold. Miss D.'s been on the phone all morning trying to find us a suitable abode. I don't know what we'll do. If she can't find one, we may have to move in with you and Carey." Then Mammie really begins crying.

"Big Alice, I'm teasing. We'll be fine. Won't we, Little Alice?" Homer spies my report card and makes a grab for it.

"The nuns used to say this card follows you the rest of your life," says Homer. "But I always got perfect A's. Let's see. . . . Oh no, this is a disaster. This is a catastrophe. This is the worst report card I've ever seen. Big Alice, this must be a mistake. There must be another Alice Carey in that dreadful school."

Now I start crying along with Mammie. Even Homer croaks up a few crocodile boo-hoos.

"No, no, it's me. It's my failure. I did it to myself and I feel awful. I hate St. Michael's. I hate the nuns. I hate the girls. I'm learning nothing. They make fun of me because I'm Irish."

"But Alice M'rie, ye've lost yer brogue."

The poison has started to seep out. I weep bitterly. I know I've broken my mammie's heart.

"Mammie, I'm sorry. I'm sorry I failed you. And now we're being evicted from here as well. God's punishing us. That's the truth. What'll happen to us? Where'll we go? We'll be homeless."

"Dwa-lings, Miss D. is dying to move."

"But where will we go? What'll we do without Gristede's?

"Alice M'rie, where will ye go? Carey'll skin us alive when he finds out ye've failed. And he'll blame me."

Bang! goes the kettle. Miss D. calls down the stairs, "Homer, I need you."

"In a minute, Jean."

He calls her Jean! He's never done that in his life. So, never one to miss a trick, *clack-clacking* down the kitchen stairs comes Miss D. in full cocktail regalia.

"Big Alice, are you all right? There's such a racket down here."

Enthusiastic in my sorrow, I blurt out, "O Miss D., I wish we didn't have to move. This is my favorite house in the entire wide world."

"Little Alice, we're moving right across the street from City Center. We'll have a doorman, a handyman, and it will be easier for Big Alice. Now, what happened?"

Homer solemnly hands Miss D. my report card, but without her glasses she can't see the terrible details.

"I don't understand high school at all," she murmurs. "I was privately educated at home by tutors, and Jed was doing such a good job with you. Little Alice, if you stayed home and read more . . . Well, I don't know anything about children."

Mammie and I say nothing to Carey. And he doesn't ask. My first year of high school is down the drain. I've won a Pyrrhic victory. I'll never have to walk across Thirty-fourth Street to St. Michael's again. Then again, I have no school to walk to, since we can't figure out where I could go to summer school. I could go to LICE, but we don't want to give Carey the satisfaction.

Mammie and I spend the summer packing up Miss D.'s house. There are boxes for the country, and boxes for the new and smaller apartment. I traipse around, touching walls I'll never see again. My sweet little room with the fractured mirror and the fur throw is disbanded. Mammie says the throw will look nice on the bottom of Miss D.'s bed in the country. Issues of *Theatre World*, *Look*, and *Playbill* are boxed and sent to Miss D.'s new office in City Center. The office boys are let go. Now it will be just Homer and Miss D.

Every day Mammie trots over to the new building to supervise the painters. We're duplicating East on West on a smaller scale. I pack up the china cats. They're building a special mantel for them in the new

227

apartment. September is almost upon us, and I don't know if I'll ever go back to school again. The move is completely absorbing Mammie and me, for in some way, it's our move, too. Mammie gets us a few days' work with Jack Richardson, the playwright. She hopes that if he likes us, I can work for him as a maid. But it doesn't pan out.

Miss D. holds down the fort in her room right up to the very end. It's the last room to be dismantled. Mammie goes to Gristede's to say good-bye. They tell her they'll deliver. But Mammie likes to chat with her butchers. We'll have to find someplace else.

I feel chastened. I've won but I've lost. I've hurt my mammie. I've lost my spark. I'm getting more pimples, too.

One day in late August, Homer suggests the three of us walk over to Fifth Avenue to take a look at a small private high school called Rhodes. He knows the headmaster. Mammie protests.

"I'm at my wit's end. I don't know what we'll do for money."

"Mammie, I'll get a part-time job."

"Sure, what can ye do? Ye can't type. Ye'll have to clean."

"Ladies," says Homer, "this is not *Stella Dallas*."

We silently walk crosstown, Mammie in black, mourning for her life, me in a Susan Strasberg.

Rhodes is in a brownstone. This perks Mammie up. Robert Lowrance, the headmaster, wears a blazer and a gold-crest pinkie ring and talks with a Texas twang. He says he understands what's happened to me. Homer and he talk. Mammie and I wait outside. We don't talk. Mr. Lowrance wants to know if I'll take an IQ test. I'll take anything. The school looks nice. It's coed. The boys wear jackets. Some of the girls look beatnik. I take the IQ test. And I'm in.

For the first time in years, I'm happy. I've an English teacher who has us reading Max Beerbohm. I thought only Jed knew about people like him. And no one laughs at me. I never cut classes.

I don't know how Mammie is paying for Rhodes. Maybe Homer is helping out. Maybe Jed. Maybe Miss D. Certainly not Carey. We told him a terrible lie. Said St. Michael's had closed down, and I'm in Rhodes because it's nearer to where Miss D. has moved. I do filing in the principal's office, which defrays some of the tuition. And for the first time in my life, I've decided to shut up and enjoy my luck.

Then, just when everything settles down, our landlady in Astoria says we must get out. She needs our apartment for her son. Carey goes nuts. Says we'll have to go on welfare. Gets into a huge fight with the woman. Calls her an "old whoor"—not fit to wipe his boots. She says we've a month to get out.

We delve into the *Long Island Star* apartment listings. I suggest to Mammie that maybe we should go Home. But we can't. What would two grown women do over there?

229

Every night after dinner Carey, Mammie, and I look at apartments in Woodside, Jamaica, Sunnyside, and Maspeth, Queens. They're always the top floor of two-family houses, freshly painted and stinking of it. Some don't want pets.

"Good," says Carey.

"But what about Mitzi, Mammie?"

She says nothing, so ashamed is my mammie to be standing in an apartment in Maspeth, owned by people not half as cultured as she. Even the view out the back windows hurts her. In the backyards there are red autumn roses and purple roses of Sharon.

I can see it in her eyes: Flowers on this land will always belong to the landlord. Once again we'll be renters, not owners.

Time is running out. I hear them in bed at night. "But D., isn't there any way we could buy something?"

"If we had the money we wasted on that one in there, we could. We're broke on account of her."

I put my good ear to the pillow. The one Carey hasn't recently banged.

By a stroke of luck, Mammie sees an ad for an apartment just down the block, and nearer the Con Edison gas tanks. Gus the Greek and his wife, Aphrodite, are renting their ground floor. We'd have access to the yard. Mammie offers to clean the halls and sweep.

"Why, a fine woman like Aphrodite shouldn't be doing that sort of thing," she tells Gus. She gets the rent down a bit and we're in.

We move by hand, Mammie, Carey, and me, lugging beds and chairs across the street and down the block. Carey's busy laughing at Gus and his wife.

"Aphro who? They'll keep her out of heaven with a name like that."

On our first Sunday we hear Gus padding down the stairs.

"Mrs., Mrs.," he says, holding out a plate of Greek cookies and a little glass of ouzo. "Old Greek custom, Mr. Denis, always honor the woman. She is goddess of the hearth." Then he gives Mammie the cookies and ouzo as a welcome gift.

Carey dined out on that for days.

"Ooooozo, ooooozo! Did ye ever hear a t'ing like that in yer life?"

We ignore him. It's the nicest thing anyone's done for my mammie in a long time.

i hear lake water lapping
with low sounds by
the shore

WHEN I'VE BEEN BY MYSELF for a while and need a city fix, I take the bus up to Cork City for a ramble-about.

I've been trying to find out if what Mammie said was true, that the Slatterys are related to Nanno Nagle. I always believed her. We all believed her. It's only recently I found out this wasn't the case. Not that Mammie was lying. It was a delusion of grandeur.

A while back, Geoffrey and I visited the Nanno Nagle Center in Ballygriffin, County Cork, near the Nagle Mountains. Two old nuns wearing cardigans, Sister Joseph and Sister Anthony (Joseph and Anthony, as they called themselves), made me smile by talking about Nanno as if they knew her personally.

"Oh, she was a wild child. Wild! Wouldn't you say, Joseph? Her father used to say, 'Oh, my Nanno will be a saint yet.'"

In the convent kitchen, over Nescafé and the best fruitcake I've ever eaten, they told me Nanno wasn't even on the first rung of the ladder to Beatification, much less a saint.

"Girl," said Joseph as we headed to the chapel, "you better start praying right *now* that they beatify

Nanno before the turn of the century. I'm afraid John Paul [as they called the Pope] is closing his eyes to poor old Ireland."

The Sisters said Nanno's grave was on the south side of the city, Cork being divided by the River Lee, much as Dublin is divided by the Liffey. The south side is filled with narrow medieval lanes lined with nineteenth-century artisans cottages, many of which dead-end on tiny squares filled with kids playing stickball. I could have asked directions, but I found it more pleasurable being lost and discovering my newly adopted city, the second largest in Ireland.

The South Presentation Convent, where Nanno Nagle is buried, is up a hill on a bustling street. The gate is open, dark and unattended. I walk up worn stone steps that hug the side of an Ursuline convent built in 1776, and enter a small walled graveyard filled with neat rows of identical white headstones marking the lives and deaths of more than a hundred nuns.

At the entrance I find the crypt containing the small oak coffin of Nanno Nagle. Across the graveyard an eighteenth-century slab of granite tells her tale:

Here lie waiting, 'tis hoped, a glorious resurrection the remains of Miss Nagle . . . departed this life, envied by many & regretted by all, on the 26th day of April 1784, aged 65 years.

There is a pretty view over the rooftops to the north side of the city and the clock tower of St. Anne's Anglican Church, with its weather vane of a gold salmon. Were it a little warmer, I might lie on a bench and take a nap. Everything is so green, so quiet, so comfy, so gray, so beautiful, so isolated. I don't want the aura broken by the arrival of someone popping in wanting to chat. But I'm left alone. It's just me, Nanno, and, I suppose, Mammie.

I start reading the stones, postmodern in their minimalism. Here's Sister de Sales Gleeson, who died this past June, sixty-two years a nun. A few red roses mark the spot. Here's Mary Connell, who became Sister Mary Joseph in April 1785 and died four short months later. Rose Healy, who became Sister Dorothy Clare, died in 1890 at age twenty-three. These are humble women who followed Nanno Nagle, a rich girl from Cork who left home to serve the poor.

The word "serve" sticks in my craw. Didn't Mammie's sister, poor Mollie, leave Carrigeen around the time of the first World War to go to Scotland to become Sister Mary Agatha? Didn't she, too, serve? Though I don't know in what capacity; Mammie never told me. And didn't she die of leukemia?

Didn't my mammie serve as well? And look what happened to her. A great sadness comes over me. Nanno still not a saint. Mammie dead. And me in Ireland trying to figure it all out. O Alice M'rie, more's the pity. Standing there wiping your nose on your sleeve and boo-hooing for your mammie, and Nanno, forgotten by all but a handful of nuns.

It's now midday. Fellow Corkonians and I are eating lunch at the English Markets. In the midst of produce stalls selling Ballycotton potatoes, local strawberries, buttered eggs, glistening fresh fish, blood pudding, and free-range chickens, people are tucking into curries, gumbos, chillies, crispy bread, green salads, and wine. There's not a fry to be had. I stand at a little bar, bearing the unlikely name of Iago, and down a plate of freshly made pasta slathered with pesto and a glass of white wine.

"Ee'ra greasy guinea food," Carey'd say.

This is the new Ireland, I say. We now have spaghetti in Cork.

"Feast your eyes, girl, feast your eyes," says Pat O'Connell, the master fishermonger, as he guts me a fresh turbot. "And where's himself?"

I love when Geoffrey is referred to as "himself."

I pass the orange-green-blue-gold enamel fountain that's been spurting away since Victoria was queen, and I see my mammie with a Savoy cabbage in her hand. Back in Carrigeen, it was a big deal to take a day and go "up to Cork." Now I call Cork my city.

The smell of hops coming from the Beamish and Crawford Brewery perfumes the noon air as I cross over the River Lee on my way back for another look at Nanno's grave. You know, I have never visited my mammie's grave. Again, I sit and look at the hundred white headstones being slowly whittled away by the damp Irish weather.

I think of all the men whose ashes we tossed into the sea at Fire Island. How, while they waited to die from AIDS, they specifically requested the ocean as their place of burial. How we'd troop down the beach—sometimes a group, sometimes just Geoffrey and me—holding a small white box heavy with the remains of a friend. How we'd swim out beyond the breakers to empty the box. And how sad it became when it dawned on me that swimming in the ocean wasn't just swimming anymore. It was swimming with the dead.

Maybe these nuns are right, being buried here for the likes of me to sit and ponder.

Eventually I hire an Irish genealogist to investigate my hoped-for relationship to Nanno. But it doesn't pan out. Nanno Nagle is not my distant cousin. My eighteenth- and nineteenth-century Slattery cousins were either spinsters or farmers. I feel cheated. Perhaps delusions of grandeur are inherited. I still believe I am related to a saint.

I'M OFTEN ALONE IN THE STABLES because Geoffrey must stay and work in New York. And sometimes I am afraid to be here by myself. Sophie du Plantier's murder remains unsolved. Gossip has it that the Garda—the Irish police—know who did it but have too little evidence to make an arrest. Yet my fear doesn't stop my wanting to be in Ireland. I am learning about the Irish: their sense of family, sense of blood, sense of community. And I hope they're learning about me.

Those small exchanges in Bantry may help them see women in a different light.

"So ye're here by yerself again."

"I am. Geoffrey's coming in a few days."

"And ye're not afraid?"

"I'm grand."

It is what I say. It's important for me to be brave.

Still and all, I've had a few new frights. One summer night I'm dead out in the bed with Thomasina when I hear the clatter of hooves. Thomasina sits up and, taking my cue from her, I do too. The night is pitch black. Yet I'm afraid to put on the light, lest I draw attention to the house and myself inside it. It's clear there are hooves thundering up the laneway. The nearer they get, the more paralyzed I become.

Suddenly the noise stops, reverses, and thunders away. Then I recognize it. It's motorcycles. Given the choice, I'd rather deal with hooves. As the noise recedes, I hear the motorcycles heading toward Schull.

I call Geoffrey, but it's only ten o'clock at night in New York, and he's not home yet. If this had happened to Mammie, or to Audrey or Sally Johnston (but it wouldn't, for they'd never be here alone), they'd have made a cup of tea. But I have a small whiskey; Thomasina, an offering of Sheba.

I decide that I must, right now, protect myself from bikers, marauders, *The Wild Bunch*, Marlon Brando, murderers, the Black and Tans, the Provos, the IRA, randy farmers, pedophile priests, Captain Billy and Wyatt, skinheads, salesmen, tinkers, and itinerants. Then I realize what probably stopped the bikers was our newly installed cow gate, designed to keep the cows off our property.

Flashlight in hand, I gird my loins and go outside for a look about. The night is still. The air is sweet. In a panic, I realize that all I have at hand to block the gate and protect myself from the bikers coming back is a wheelbarrow full of sod, branches, stones, and weeds.

I wheel the barrow down to the gate. Quietly, quietly. Keep the girls from bellowing. They know me. They like me. I hear them moving toward me in the pasture. I mustn't confuse John and Audrey into thinking there are prowlers on the laneway. They'd want to help, they'd be up in a flash. Then they'd see me trying to defend myself with a wheelbarrow, and I'd be embarrassed.

I double the weight of the barrow with more rocks and debris. I open the gate and wheel the barrow to the other side. However, when I try to go back to my side, I can't. The barrow is interfering with the way the gate swings. I've only succeeded in shutting myself out. The girls are hovering, staring at me, munching their hay. They are admiring my muslin Victorian nightgown. Now

I realize the only way I can bring the evening's adventure to a safe close is to climb over the cow gate. Then I can go home.

Home, Alice M'rie.

And I do. In dawn's early light, with my skirts knotted up around me, I look like a girl in a Watteau painting.

The next day Audrey tells me that over the years, summer bikers have used the Big House as an impromptu campsite. Still, I buy a thick chain with a sturdy padlock to lock myself away from demons new and unknown to my New York savvy.

I was alone in Ireland on August 15, 1998, when an IRA spin-off, calling itself "the Real IRA," planted a car bomb in a street crowded with Saturday shoppers in Omagh, County Tyrone, killing thirty-two people, Catholic and Protestant alike, and injuring more than a hundred.

I had just arrived at Faileth Not from New York when Audrey Johnston rang to tell me Thomasina had moved in, she thought, with new neighbors, the Jamisons, who had bought a nearby derelict house. I was down at the Johnstons' getting details of Thomasina's defection when the bulletin about the bombing came on television. It was 3:20 on a glorious summer afternoon. In an instant, the Good Friday Peace Agreement had been rent asunder.

As I walked back up our laneway, pitifully calling out, "Thomasina, Thomasina," I realized I identified with both victim and terrorist. I thought of Carey, how the only time he ever touched me was with his fists. And how I, too, would react that way when sad, angry, or frustrated. When I get needy, I get mean. That neediness, though never acknowledged in words, for words are weak, brought about many a violent confrontation between Geoffrey and myself in what we now refer to as "the old days."

Now we can laugh at our behavior, especially when another couple proudly tells us they never fight. We'll even volunteer stories. Especially the one where I threw a heavy cast-iron frying pan of veal cutlets at Geoffrey that hit his leg (the scar is still there) and landed upside down on the floor. Anger exploding in a crash of meat, lemons, wine, and butter. I rescued the cutlets, reheated them. And we ate them in bitter silence.

At the time it felt fine to behave that way. It was the only way I knew how to behave. Carey didn't talk with me or to me. If he said anything at all, it was to mock. To cut. To demean. To kill a laugh. To raise a welt. And Mammie said nothing. She must have been terrified of him. Too terrified to come to my aid.

Yet here I am in Ireland, crying real tears because my cat has defected to another house. And crying because of my Irishness in an Ireland that never gives up its old hatreds.

Day turns into evening, and I am walking the fields. In Omagh the body count is rising. They say Prince

Charles is about to make a visit. The sky is Corsican blue. And Thomasina is nowhere to be found. I have not yet met the Jamisons. I know I must go down there, introduce myself, and see if my cat is there. So what if I look like a fool.

"Thomasina, Thomasina," I call into the wind; but she doesn't respond.

The Jamisons' house, abandoned for years like our own, is buzzing with activity. I stand near a crumbling ruin of a tumbled cottage, quite like the ones on our land, and call out, "Hello, it's Alice Carey. I'm your neighbor. I'm looking for my cat."

David Jamison appears. He looks like an artistic stevedore. "Have a Scotch," he says. "It's been a terrible day."

Thomasina is inside the house holding court, accepting kisses and acting like a coquette. And there am I, with the Jamisons' large, extended, Protestant family, who have traveled from County Down in the North to help them get settled. Everyone is having a cocktail, but the getting-to-know-you process is unimportant, for we're all listening to the body count in Omagh.

Peace. The Peace Accord. The Peace Agreement. The Peace Referendum. The Good Friday Agreement. Give Peace a Chance. Words, only words. Palaver.

When I walk back to Faileth Not, Thomasina stays with the Jamisons. I cannot sleep that night, nor for the next five, until Geoffrey arrives. Once again the violence in Ireland has cast a pall over me and over this house. I'm scared to be alone here. I can't get Carey's mocking laugh out of my head, nor his yellow teeth grinning at me in gleeful anger. Sophie du Plantier's murderer is prowling laneways looking for victims. Those bikers are on the road. And now Omagh.

Every day I visit the Jamisons. Sometimes Thomasina walks back with me, demanding milk. Some nights she falls asleep here on her chair, only for me to rise in the morning to find her gone.

I fixate on Carey's violence, wondering what it would have been like not to have been banged around as a child. It's taken years for me to squelch my own need to hurt, to jibe, to make a smart crack, just like him. Years to learn to listen. Yet without my old hard edge, I feel powerless.

I don't know how Carey felt. Something must have happened years ago when he was one of eleven kids up there in the mountains. Something must have made him feel that the only way he'd be heard was to strike out. I sometimes joke with Geoffrey that I've "gotten terribly Zen about everything." I try. And sometimes it works. At least I try not to hurt anyone, including myself.

I distract myself by going up to the Big House to envision what it will look like when Geoffrey and I do it up. We want it to be a traditionally painted Georgian house, with a courtyard herb garden and a cutting garden. Even vegetables. Yet I undermine this vision by taking a portable radio with me to hear about Omagh.

I've become nutty with fear. I tell myself I am brave. I don't have to lock the cow gate at night. Those bikers will not return. Sophie's murderer will not seek me out.

I have chosen to be here in Ireland, a place where beauty and violence coexist. Our property, with its tumbled Catholic dwellings and Protestant Big House, stands as witness to the schism brought on by religion.

So I walk the fields again, hoping Thomasina will join me, and I wind up at the Jamisons'. They have started to uncover an old, old apple orchard, hidden for years behind their house under brambles and trees.

Aidan, their son, and I pick apples. He's in his twenties. I think, had Geoffrey and I chosen to have children, they would now be Aidan's age.

"Are you a Catholic?" he asks.

"I suppose so," I say.

"And Geoffrey?"

"He's Protestant."

"That's hard, then, isn't it?"

And I smile. "It is, sometimes. But we've stayed together."

I tell him that Geoffrey loves to bake, and when he gets here, he'll make his specialty, an American apple pie with a lattice crust.

Aidan and I walk around this thicket of ancient trees frosted with lichen and dripping small green apples with red blushes. Then Thomasina (with an insouciance known only to cats) dashes down from the Ring Fort.

We walk, the three of us, back to Faileth Not. In New York, Geoffrey is getting on a plane. He'll be here in the morning.

"She's decided to stay," says Aidan as Thomasina settles down in her chair. He's right. And at least temporarily, peace is restored for me.

While i stand on
the roadway

I WAS PLANNING TO WEAR Mammie's linen dress for our housewarming. It was the day Princess Diana was killed.

It's eight-fifteen in the morning on a rainy August Sunday. We have guests, John and Larry, from New York. And by three o'clock the place will be packed with neighbors and friends, all invited to raise a glass and christen these stables Faileth Not. Coffee perks on the AGA. The tea is in the pot. Brown bread is sliced. We turn on BBC Radio for the news.

"Diana, Princess of Wales"—we pay no attention—"was killed in a car accident. . . ." The cow-still silence cracks. "No, no, no, no! It's not fair! It's not fair!" I wail. "She can't die."

John and Larry stare at their oatmeal. No scenes, please, no scenes. I can read it on their foreheads. I can't blame them. They're on holiday.

The delicate, thin-lipped china cup I hold in my hand is covered in pink roses. It was given to Geoffrey and me as a wedding gift. I caress this little cup, bursting with English roses, and want to dash it on the ground to ease my rage. But I don't. I can't. I can't make a scene. I can't break a cup I love because a woman I *love—like? admire? what?*—has been killed.

The BBC repeats its mantra again and again. Princess Diana . . . was killed. Was killed. Was killed. In Paris, with her companion, Dodi Fayed.

Diana of the hunt, caught under the Seine in the middle of the night running from the paparazzi. Geoffrey turns on the TV. Every station is running the black-and-white security film of Dodi and Diana leaving the Ritz through a revolving door.

Every few minutes I start in. *It's not fair. It's not fair.* I exchange my cup for an ordinary one, suitable for breaking. Yet I don't break it. John and Larry are the ballast. I can't disgrace myself. Were I alone, I could go mad. I catch Geoffrey looking at me, knowing this is true.

A full Irish breakfast, right down to the blood pudding, is served up in silence. John and Larry tuck in.

"Got to keep our strength up," says Larry.

Strength indeed. Strength to put up with a wailing woman. I feel embarrassed. My violent reaction surprises me. Even in a darkened cinema, when everyone around me is crying because Dorothy wants to go home to Kansas, I hold it in. I can't lose my dignity. Stiff upper lip. That's what Mammie'd want.

The phone rings and rings again. New York calling: Do you know anything different? You're lucky to have the BBC! Maybe it's all a mistake. You know how the French are. Outside, the pathetic fallacy weeps on the flagstones.

Were we on Fire Island, we'd cancel the party. Queens would don black armbands and initiate morning

249

cocktails in Diana's honor. House flags would fly at half mast. But not only are we in Ireland, we are in the heart of the country. People have already started out, some driving from miles away to be with us to christen this house.

Killed in a car crash. Just like that. Just like my mammie. Killed by a car. My mammie left there like a bag of garbage, on the street. Two women crushed upon impact. Diana wearing white linen; my mammie, a tan raincoat.

The BBC speaks with the voice of authority.

"We have no more details."

Yet they continue to run the security footage. It's not fair it's not fair it's not fair. Geoffrey turns off the TV and puts on Sinatra.

In a burst of synchronicity, I realize I've readied myself to mourn Diana. Only yesterday, I bought a pair of jet Victorian mourning earrings.

"Oh, yes," purred Tim, the antique shop's owner, "people have been looking at these earrings all summer, but no one has had the style to buy them but you." Here I was thinking them merely pretty. I never thought I'd have to wear them in mourning.

Party time approaches. Prince Charles's plane touches down in Paris. John and Larry drive to the bakery to pick up the cake. I poach a salmon. Wash wineglasses. Slice lemons. Set up tea trays. The weather's clearing up. I can't get Mammie out of my head. For this event, this baptism of our ruin, I'm going to wear her dress. The one

Carey missed in his auto-da-fé after her death, because it was rolled in a ball in the back of a drawer.

The dress is a buttercup-yellow 1930s shift made by hand, perhaps by Mammie herself. Perhaps she had a hidden talent for sewing, a talent she found too Irish, too poor, too countrified to reveal. Yet she darned socks, hemmed skirts, and taught me to do the same. She also said good dresses were best bought at Bonwit Teller.

I concentrate on the dress, the earrings, the black cashmere sweater. This is proper mourning attire to salute two women who died impeccably dressed.

By four o'clock, the house is packed with people wanting to be here, yet under the circumstances feeling a little odd about it. The usual comments are bandied about. Oh, it's just as well. She couldn't have married him. Look how the royals treated Princess Margaret and the Duchess of Windsor. Elaine Johnston wants to know, had I seen Diana's wedding on TV? I hadn't. The day Diana married Charles, Geoffrey and I were walking around Venice embarking on our own romance.

Geoffrey and I salute one and all who helped us create this house. But I neither eat nor drink. I miss my mother. As soon as people leave I want a drink to ease the pain. But Geoffrey stills my hand.

"You can do what you want to, but . . ." (Geoffrey being a great one for "buts" and "consequences").

Wineless I sit, looking down the lane to the hills that separate Faileth Not from Kerry, where Mammie was born.

To ease the pain I start playing songs in my head, just like I did at her funeral.

THROUGH THE WHOLE of Mammie's funeral, the Beatles song "Penny Lane" plays in my head. It's my distraction from Carey while we sit by ourselves in the front row of the Mac waiting for Mass to begin. It's a Thursday in December 1967, and "Penny Lane is in my ears and in my eyes."

Shifting my legs from the nearness of Carey's knees, I let my eyes wander around this Mission-style horror of a Catholic church, and I know why I fled from home only four months before.

There beneath the blue suburban skies

Two days ago my mammie was clipped by a hit-and-run driver as she dashed home to make Carey's morning tea, after cooking up a "fry" for the old Irish pensioners down the way. She did things like that. She'd take on the damnedest people, as if she didn't have enough to do tending Carey and Jed and Miss D.

Ten to ten. O'Shea, the funeral director from next door, has hustled the mourners out too early and into the church. Bet he has another coffin waiting in the wings.

"O'Shea'll give ye a great send-off. Better him than them Guinzos down the way." That's Carey's opinion of the local undertakers. Now he really knows.

In her pink suit she is. Her Jackie Kennedy suit. But no hat. I picked out her eggshell-white straw hat, with little beauty marks strewn across the veil. But O'Shea said no.

"Hats aren't worn in coffins."

"Mammie wore hats all the time."

"It's just not done."

And so she isn't. Nor is she carrying her pocketbook, or wearing gloves. Just a rosary twined round her fingers.

So toil worn for me
Ah, bless you and keep you,
Mother Macree

Hateful song. Irish American sentimentality.

Carey and I are sitting in a church I'll never return to, whilst my mammie's lying next door in a cheap plywood coffin covered in Mother Mary blue damask.

I could have knelt down and said a prayer, damn it. I could have gone in to take a look at her and see if the suit looked all right. But I didn't. I couldn't. I spent the night of the wake in O'Shea's office with my girlfriend Dianne, eating a box of chocolates we found in his desk.

Wasn't it only a week ago Mammie and I were looking at the Rockefeller Center Christmas tree? I met her at Miss D.'s. She said she wanted to walk over and see the Christmas lights. She was going on about a wake she'd just gone to at O'Shea's, and I was telling her I never again wanted to look at anyone dead in a coffin. Mammie was laughing. "Ye go for the gossip," she said.

I should have checked to see if the cheap coffin really looked cheap. Plywood rots faster than mahogany.

Two to ten. O'Shea and the pallbearers are late. They should be in the back of the church by now. Blame it on the solstice. It is the shortest day of the year.

Sitting behind Carey and me are pews full of weeping neighbors, their eyes glued on us. I can feel them burning a hole in my hennaed head. Mrs. Scott. Mrs. Jackson. Mrs. Trainor. Mrs. Kelly. I can smell Mrs. Donovan's Camel cigarettes. Lily McCann's snuff. The cold of the church holds the smell.

Miss D.'s here, too. I can smell her Blue Grass perfume. Bet she's wearing her little mink and those thrup'ny-bit heels. I'd like to know who made her tea this morning. Someone'll have to learn to boil water.

A Janus image they were, Mammie and Miss D. Connected by airs. Set apart by class and money.

The General is with Miss D., all decked out in his Korean War hero's uniform. That'll cause a stir among the populace. And Jed is hunched up in the back row. I hear him coughing. I can smell his Salems hovering in the air.

But it's Homer who's running the show. Since he's always dead set on style and ritual, Homer is standing in the back of the church greeting people. He even called me up at six this morning with a style tip.

"Dwa-linggggg . . . you must err on the side of chic for Big Alice's High Mass. The weather will be warm enough for your peach coat."

And I'm wearing it. I'm the only one not dressed in black or mink.

My mammie's dead. Dead to begin with. Killed in the midst of doing a good deed. If I had a dime for every Horn & Hardart fruitcake she gave the old ladies, or the Sunday supplements she mailed back to Ireland, or the bags of groceries she lugged for sick neighbors, or the hundreds of nylons she washed out in the basin by hand for Miss D., I'd have enough money to send her body back to Ireland. She might have wanted that. I don't know. She didn't say.

People will always remember she died in the street. That's a sight that sticks. Legs askew. Hat off. Spilt milk. Don't cry after. Always helping others. Sometimes me. Never herself. Always Carey, who never appreciated her. Sitting beside him right now is the closest I've been to him in years.

Mrs. Pelleteri's waving at me. She's pointing at my coat. Yes, it is nice. I bet she's made the connection that Mammie's in pink and I'm in peach.

Penny Lane. Liverpool. Killarney. Astoria. All the same thing. John Lennon said the Beatles were more popular than Jesus Christ. But God is dead. To have my mammie die in the street like that . . .

Broke her heart I did. She stayed in bed the whole weekend I moved out last September. Now she was stuck in Astoria with Carey. Oh, we patched it up a bit. She came down to my flat in Greenwich Village a few times with corn muffins and tuna fish. But things were never the same again.

Three minutes past ten. Maybe it's all a joke. I bet she's gotten up out of that cheap coffin and is over across the street, banging on the Deutsch Brothers door looking for some lamb chops. But no, she's not. The Deutsch brothers are there in the back row. Dave, Joe, and Jack are wearing yarmulkes. They've closed the store in Mammie's honor.

Neighborhood women, members of the Rosary Society, line the aisle awaiting her coffin.

The family that prays together stays together.

Their motto. Not ours. We didn't. Couldn't. We didn't even go to Mass together.

Carey's mute. He must know Mammie took the back way, the shortcut home, to avoid his seeing her. To avoid his judgment and possibly his hand. The pensioners she'd gone to cook breakfast for rang up to say they'll be praying the Mass along with Father Lyons.

"We'll get yer mammie into heaven. Don't ye worry."

Everyone's standing. It's really happening. Mammie is not buying chops. Father Lyons, all dressed up in high black drag, is in position. He's the old bastard whom I confessed that sin of impurity to when I was ten. Ten!

The organ's wheezing out the Mass for the Dead. Black was Mammie's favorite color. Maybe she should be wearing her black suit, not that pink one. Dreary music. They should be playing something from one of Miss D.'s shows.

The Rosary Society, led by Alice Bray, turns and faces the door. Hadn't I just yelled at the old bitch in the back of the church?

Shouldn't have done that. Shouldn't have yelled at old Alice Bray. All she did was remind me of the importance of the rosary. But all the rosaries in the world didn't stop that car from hitting my mammie. Homer pulled me away from her. She'll chalk it up to grief.

"You miss your mammie," she said.

My mammie didn't give two shites about the rosary, or novenas, or any of that hocus-pocus going on up there. What she cared about were properly ironed hems. Red lipstick. My posture. Tuna fish sandwiches. A pot of tea with honey in a blue pitcher, mind. And that I'd turn out to be a Lady. A Lady. Not a Paddy. Not a greenhorn. Not a narrow-back. But a Lady. And a New Yorker.

And I am.

A lady wearing a peach melton coat with a wraparound belt from Bendel's. Bendel's, I tell you, not Gimbel's. Not Macy's. But Henri Bendel's on Fifty-seventh Street. The store I lied about, in an attempt to glamorize Mammie's death. For years after her death, I would tell people the car knocked her down in front of

Bendel's. I didn't want her dead in some side street by the Astoria gas tanks.

Signal given, the Rosarians raise their arms to heaven. Fingers touching. Rosary beads jingling. The world as I knew it changes utterly as I stand to watch the coffin of my mammie, Alice Slattery Carey, slide up the aisle on her way to heaven.

SYNCHRONICITY IS AN ODD THING. During Princess Diana's funeral in Westminster Abbey, I planted a peach-colored rose in her honor. I am kneeling in the border garden, preparing the ground, and watching through the open French doors as Prime Minister Tony Blair, on TV, reads from the First Epistle of St. Paul to the Corinthians. Faileth Not, the name we christened the stables, is interpolated from this letter.

"'If I speak with the tongues of men, and of angels, and have not charity, I am become as sounding brass, or a tinkling cymbal.'"

As Blair continues speaking, I dig into the Irish soil to plant an English rose.

"'Charity suffereth long, and is kind.'"

The day is hot. My hair keeps falling in my face. I keep brushing it away with muddy hands that only serve to smear dirt on my face. And I'm crying, not so much for my mammie or Diana, but for my old self—the girl who wore a peach-colored coat to her mammie's funeral.

258

"'Charity . . . beareth all things, believeth all things, hopeth all things, endureth all things. . . .'"

It's hard to concentrate with the heat and the late-summer flies. I am a little ashamed of myself for reacting this way to a woman who was a media phenomenon and a princess, someone I'd never really thought of before except to admire her spunk. Yet here I am crying and focusing on every word of Diana's funeral while I barely was present in spirit at my own mother's.

Blair continues, "'Charity never faileth. . . . When I was a child, I spake as a child, I understood as a child, I thought as a child. But when I became a man, I put away childish things.'"

I think of Mammie and me back there at the Winter Garden Theater at *Peter Pan*, watching this boy who doesn't want to grow up. How I'd play the album in my bedroom in Astoria over and over again. How I loved the song Peter sings with the Lost Boys, "I Won't Grow Up." How the Lost Boys were bound together in believing that "growing up is awfuler than all the awful things that ever were." And how one night I must have had a bad dream and woke up in a panic.

"Mammie, Mammie," I cried out. Mammie came in and sat on my bed. I was embarrassed even back then, for crying was not good form. "Mammie," I said, trying to cover my tears. "I'm afraid to grow up . . . you know, like the song."

"I know," she said. And we sat in silence. "I know."

Or on the pavements grey

THE STABLES ARE WARMED. Christened. With my finger, I scrape the last smidgens of icing from the cake box. Then we wash up the wineglasses. As Prince Charles's plane touches down in Paris, Geoffrey and I put a moratorium on watching any more of the proceedings on the TV. Only then does a sense of calm settle over our house on this bittersweet August evening.

We decide to drive into Bantry and take John and Larry for a walk around the bay. In New York our differences would not be so apparent, but in Ireland I see what an eclectic mix we are as couples; Geoffrey and I, a Protestant living with a Catholic; John and Larry, a Mormon with a Jew. Yet here we are together in Ireland on this hay-scented evening. Four unique people in harmony with one another.

I begin to tell them about Astoria in the fifties and how the first people I ever recognized as different from Mammie and Carey and me were Jewish: the Deutsch brothers and the Kleins, our downstairs neighbors.

It's around 1957 and I'm down in the landlord's yard looking up at the window of our new neighbors,

Jewish immigrants from Israel. Leah is in her kitchen making soup. Morris is leaning out the window smoking. Eva, their six-year-old daughter, is trotting downstairs for the English lesson I'm about to give her. *The Heart Is a Lonely Hunter* hasn't worked as a reader, and I've found something better in the library.

I'm sitting under my lovely cherry tree reading the library book. Carey's probably asleep on the couch. Mammie's banging chops in the pan. Leah leans her boo-sams out the window.

"Eva . . . *somethingsomethingsomething Hebrew* . . . don't *something–something* bother Aleeze."

"No, no. It's no bother, Mrs. Klein. I love teaching Eva to read. And I've got the book to do the trick, *Pegeen of Bantry Bay*."

Carey's head appears in the window.

"Ee'ra, what do ye want to know about Bantry Bay for?"

"D., cup of tea?" calls Mammie.

He retreats.

Eva comes out the screen door followed by Leah, who is holding a plate of little jelly cookies. I say nothing. I don't want my high-pitched brogue to disturb the serenity of this summer afternoon. Beneath my beautiful cherry tree. On this green-and-red book-filled day.

"Eva, I've a new book for you, *Pegeen of Bantry Bay*."

"Is nice?"

"It's very nice."

263

Eva takes a cookie from the plate and eats it with such dainty bites, I want to take the rest and cram them in my mouth, like Monstro the whale.

"Eva," says Leah, "pil-eeze read to Morr-ees and me."

Smiling, I take the book from Eva.

"First me. Then you. Okay?"

"Okey-dokey."

"'Once upon a time, long, long ago in old Ireland, there was a girl named Pegeen who lived by Bantry Bay.'"

Eva takes the book, looks up to Leah, who has joined Morris in a cigarette, and in a loud voice proclaims, "Once was a girl."

"Brava, Eva!" screams her mother.

Carey comes down with the garbage, assesses the scene, and looks at the Kleins.

"Ee'ra, Mrs., Alice M'rie's wastin' yer time wit' all that Irish stuff. This is America, right? Land of th' free. Home of th' brave. She should be readin' *Gone wit' d' Wind* or some story like that."

The next day, Mammie and I are shining Miss D.'s stair guards with Brasso.

"Mammie, where's Bantry Bay?"

"Cork."

"Is that near Home?"

"Alice M'rie, why be reading old things like that?"

"It's nice. It's about stuff I don't know. Pegeen lives in a thatched house with no electricity or water even."

"Alice M'rie, ye don't want to know at all about that."

Later I make sure Mammie sees me reading *A Tree Grows in Brooklyn*. But at the Astoria library I renew my new favorite book. I also take out *Gone with the Wind*. Hide one. Display the other. *Gone with the Wind* is on the coffee table. Carey doesn't even notice it. I secretly read *Pegeen of Bantry Bay* in bed at night.

I'm dying to know all about old Ireland.

"Mammie, did ye ever cook a fresh-killed goose on Michelmas?"

That was the last straw.

"Alice M'rie, I don't want ye wasting time reading stuff like that. That stuff happened long ago. No one lives that way in Ireland now."

Not one to rock the boat, I return Pegeen to the library.

OVER BANTRY BAY, the light is fading to orange. Locals are taking their evening stroll on the bay walk. Ladies with old corgis. Teens with blue hair and nose rings. New Age travelers in dreadlocks, children at their feet. Old men in tweeds with walking sticks. Young women in pastel track suits, swinging their arms while they take their power walks.

Beyond Bantry Bay, sunset is creeping down on the Beara Peninsula. All the road signs point to Kerry. And I smile. So near and yet so far.

John and Larry decide to take their car and go for a longer drive around the bay. I see Geoffrey pointing out

Bantry House to them. I know he's telling them how we stayed there the night we first saw our ruin.

Suddenly, up ahead I see a woman with a familiar strut walking a dog. Something about her gait, her hat, the cock of her head, makes me think of Mammie. I quicken my pace. People do come back from beyond the pale.

"Mammie . . ."

Mammie wouldn't be caught dead in Bantry, yet from the cut of her, this woman does look like my mammie. An old lady with a blind corgi shoots me a look. I must have said "Mammie" out loud.

I've got to see who this is. I start to trot, to run. I get up speed . . . and it is my mammie. She's walking Miss D.'s dog and wearing a new hat. A green one with feathers. Green. Not black. Not like her.

"Alice M'rie, wear black in winter, white in summer," she would say. "Nothing else'll do."

"Mammie, Mammie . . ." I dash up right behind her. "It's me, Alice M'rie."

The woman doesn't turn around. There's no bark of recognition from Chindu. Maybe she's deaf. Yet I'm positive it's her. I can tell by the tilt of her head.

"Mammie, Mammie . . . what're ye doing here?"

"Alice M'rie, what're ye doing here?"

"I'm living here, by Bantry Bay. Bantry Bay— remember?"

She doesn't get it. Her look of disapproval descends from the color of my hair to my worn Doc Martins.

266

"Alice M'rie, ye're wearing men's shoes and ye've not a hat on yer head."

"Well, look at you. This is Ireland. You're dressed for Madison Avenue."

"Chindu and I are headed for a little spin on Madison."

"Mammie, look . . . we're by Bantry Bay."

With that, the clock on St. Brendan's tolls six. The Whiddy Island ferry is coming into port. Fishermen are stowing their lobster pots for the night. For a second, everything seems normal. But nothing is normal. The lady with the blind corgi passes by without even noticing my mammie (Oh so elegantly dressed) standing by Bantry Bay in this lingering August twilight.

"Alice M'rie, far from me to be critical, but what are ye doing here? Ye never come to my grave, yet ye hop a plane to come over to Ireland."

"But Mammie, ye're buried in the Bronx . . . the Bronx. Right? New Yorkers don't go up to the Bronx. My husband and I bought an old house here. That's why I'm here."

Silence.

"Waste of money . . . Alice M'rie, I can't believe ye'd do such a thing."

"What thing?"

"I never thought ye'd get married. And I never thought ye'd be back in Ireland. Why?"

"But Mammie, don't ye remember that library book? And Eva Klein? Me teaching her to read?"

Mammie says nothing but stares over to the Kerry mountains. We've walked as far as the graveyard by the end of the road. People are putting flowers on graves. Mammie sniffs.

We turn and walk back toward Bantry. A stray dog saunters by and starts barking hysterically at nothing. Chindu has disappeared like the Cheshire cat.

"Mammie, remember me reading *Pegeen of Bantry Bay*, and how upset it got ye? Ye didn't want me to read it, but ye never said why."

"Alice M'rie, I don't remember that book at all. All I remember is ye being down there in that yard reading."

Then I start to recite: "Once upon a time, long, long ago in old Ireland, there was a girl named Pegeen who lived by Bantry Bay."

Up on the square, colored lights left over from the carnival have come on.

"Alice M'rie, look. Those lights remind me of—"

"The last time I saw ye—"

"At Rockefeller Center."

"Then you came down to my flat."

"Terrible place. That Irishman, your super."

"Mr. Sweeney was black. O Mammie, ye didn't like where I lived then and ye don't like it now. Do ye?"

"Alice M'rie, on a beautiful evening with the Duchess of Windsor giving a tea, do ye think I'd leave heaven to come down here to Bantry to tell ye I don't like what ye're doing?"

"I want to know why ye hated that book."

"Alice M'rie, I didn't want ye wasting your time reading about Ireland. I wanted ye to read about grandeur. It's bad enough we had to live in that freezing flat with Carey. I wanted ye to have something to aspire to. But ye insisted on reading about poor people in old Ireland."

"It was only a book."

"That's all it takes. Look at ye now."

Up on the square children are selling sunflowers. Cars are circling trying to find a parking spot. The chains of lights add a Mediterranean touch.

"Alice M'rie, now ye listen to me. This is not the Ireland I ran from. This is the new Ireland. Now ye've bakeries, wine stores, even supermarkets with butchers in them. People have money to burn. They aren't living in mud-walled cabins. They can even divorce. I was born too early. The stuff in that book, Alice M'rie, is what I ran from. Do ye hear me? I ran away from it with Carey. And it never did get better. I didn't want ye to know a thing about old Ireland. I wanted ye to be a real New Yorker."

"And I am, Mammie. I am. I'm a real New Yorker living in Ireland."

O'Brien's shop starts playing the theme from *The Quiet Man*, and Mammie, my mammie, looks both wondrous and different. Yet she is the same. On the other side of the square I see my Geoffrey buying a bunch of sunflowers.

And when the moonlight peeps across the
    rooftops
Of this great city, wondrous tho' it be . . .

"Alice M'rie, ye're here in Ireland. I can't get over it. Ye've come *Home*. Haven't ye?"

"Mammie, I'm not Alice M'rie anymore."

"But ye are, girl. To me."

With that, she's gone. Gone without a shower of fairy dust.

Geoffrey crosses the square toward me. He's holding out the sunflowers.

The music continues.

But tho' though they paved the footways here
    with gold dust,
I still would choose the Isle of Innisfree.

"Geoffrey," I say, "let's go home."

i hear it in the
deep heart's core

WE SOLD MAGIC FLUTE.

Before we left, we buried the animals down by the moss path.

It's the weekend before Halloween. Geoffrey is taking down Stephen's oak paneling; it's the only thing he really cares about taking. I'm going through the "summer bedroom" ('cause it's too cold to sleep there in winter), trying to figure out what to do with the stuff I can't take to Ireland.

A burglar partially solved my problem. When we returned to Magic Flute from Ireland in September, someone had broken in, camped out, and made a mess. Someone who divested me of my sillies and pretties.

But what would I do with them, anyway? Gowns, boas, gold sandals, suitable only for theme parties and gay benefits at the beach. What could I possibly do in Ireland with the manqué Holy Communion dress and veil I wore to the "Veil" party? Or the oversize Navy whites I wore to the "Stage Door Canteen" party? Or my bosom-popping Betsey Johnson bustier? Pretties. Sillies. Suitable for a costume box. Sillies I'll soon be too old to wear.

As stuff gets packed I strive to keep the house cheerful. Bunches of blue Michelmas daisies stand on a Deco sideboard bought in Lebanon, Ohio.

"Are you sure this will work in the Big House?"

"It will."

Late autumn roses, culled from the gardens of closed-for-the-season houses, perfume the Hoosier cabinet bought in Delaware.

"It'll work in the bathroom for towels and stuff."

It won't.

"It will."

The house is aglow with candles and oil lamps. But the piles of books, the bric-a-brac are all packed, and the light seems flat. There's so much stuff. Stuff firmly rooted in this island. Even the Lee Bailey cookbooks, all seven of them, which we're taking with us. I look at the inscription Geoffrey wrote to me in *Country Weekends*: "I bought this for your Bloomsday Birthday 1983 and now it's December '86. Perhaps I waited to inscribe it until we had a house of our own to have country weekends in." Little did we know.

Most of our stuff will be out of place in Ireland. I'm laying it out on my bed, the old chrome yellow bed that I love, the bed we've decided to leave for the women who bought Magic Flute.

The animals are here as well. The ragtag lot are looking at me. Dimitri, a pink Easter Bunny, who sat in an antique shop window on Bleecker Street for quite a long

273

time. Snoopy, bits 'n' pieces of his ears ripped off by cats. And Sweeney, a Golliwog from London, a present from Father Bob. He, too, nipped by said cats.

But it's Tiddly who speaks. Tiddly, whom Mammie claimed was my first toy. A present from the Murphys. He's been loved so much over the years, he's now but a small mound of cotton batting wrapped in a red silk scarf. Tiddly, whom I slept with and squeezed to death when Mammie died.

"My dear, it's time. We have served you well. Isn't it time you let us go?"

In my mind's eye I still see Tiddly as a small, red-checked gingham dog. I don't know why Mammie named him Tiddly.

Hurry up, please. It's time.

I'm pulling stuff out of drawers. Stuff from under the bed. Golden dance shoes worn in *Candide*. Tangerine slippers. A cracked pair of Joan Crawford spectator pumps. Scratched reading glasses. Single earrings. Pins without clasps. On the kitchen counter is a lineup of cracked crockery. Stuff. Stuff you keep because you loved the giver. A brown teapot with yellow roses from our neighbor Cecil, its spout now cracked, Cecil now in a nursing home. Out in the shed, muddy boots, work shirts, ski sweaters, Eric's stuff. Stuff Geoffrey got when Eric died of AIDS. Piles of stuff grow all over the house.

Geoffrey and I wander around outside. Down in the deli there is a moss path that we've cultivated for ten years. When we first bought Magic Flute, the moss was but a small patch of green. And like us, it grew.

The moss path leads to a patch of ferns and Siberian iris, where we've interred the ashes of men who died from AIDS. These are the friends who asked to be buried in our garden at Magic Flute, not tossed in the ocean. First we buried one, then another, then another. Small ceremonies. A song. A sprinkle of whiskey. In the small circle where they're buried, nothing grows.

"We can't dig 'em up and take 'em with us."

". . . and they don't want to go."

We laugh a little at the Sisyphean task of it.

"Geoffrey," I say, "let's bury the animals and stuff."

Near sunset we return to the moss path to bury parts of ourselves here on this island. Geoffrey digs a large hole in the swampy land by the lads, and I pile up our talismans.

Eric's work boots go in first, to provide a foundation. Then his ski sweater. Janie's tangerine shoes and my gold ones. Father Bob's clerical collar. An old apron of Mammie's. Cecil's teapot, a cracked cup with a tea bag. A beloved cat's food bowl. One of Geoffrey's workout shirts and his business card. Old spectacles, earrings. A Bakelite bracelet. Lastly, the animals. Snoopy holding on to Tiddly; Dimitri to Sweeney.

Hurry up please, it's time.

The October light shimmers. A ferry whistle sounds. A few deer stroll by on the boardwalk. Geoffrey and I stare at our pile of stuff. And I have to smile. The lads would be laughing at us. *It's junk . . . go have a cocktail. Haven't you anything better to do?* And they'd be right. Yet it is our junk. I sprinkle some brandy on the lot, and we just look at it. Stuff. Our stuff. Part of our life here on Fire Island. Then we hold on to each other for dear life and cry.

At sunset we take a last walk on the beach and stand looking at an October sun setting smack over the Atlantic. Down a ways we see a young couple with a dog and a small rubber boat also watching the sunset. Odd, us gazing at the sun literally setting on this part of our lives whilst a younger couple unsentimentally pull their boat up on the sand, their dog leading the way.

It starts to rain and we head back. As we sit on the couch with wine, we hear a skirmish on the kitchen deck. The deer must have wandered in. But no, David, a neighbor, with his consort, Tim—Cherry Grove's incumbent Queen of 1997. They're trick-or-treating a bit early.

What a miraculous sight is this duo dressed up as jellyfish, shimmering in the fall rain. Yards of sea-green Mylar drape their heads. Platform shoes make them giants. Tiny concealed flashlights cast light on their tentacles, the ribs of which I suspect are umbrellas.

"Trick or treat. Trick or treat . . ."

And I hoot, "Oh yes, oh yes. I have some real treats here, some Cadbury bars all the way from Cork."

Ave atque vale. The old Grove spirit bids us good-bye.

A week later, on Halloween morning, Geoffrey and I are at Faileth Not, having our morning tea. We're listening to an old duffer on the radio lay on the palaver about ghosts. He says Halloween is a Celtic feast, the beginning of spring in the underworld. While earth is bracing itself for the coming of winter, the spirits below are hot to trot. He says we should, indeed we must, welcome the dead into our homes tonight by lighting candles in the windows and keeping the fire banked for the night.

Geoffrey and I lock eyes. I see it in his, he in mine. We're both thinking of Magic Flute and how we walked out the door for the last time only a week ago today. The rain was lashing our faces, trying to wipe away our tears as we stumbled down the boardwalk for the last time on our way to the ferry.

Now we must celebrate our first Halloween in Ireland. Tonight we will light the windows of the Big House to welcome back our ghosts. There hasn't been a light in the house since 1934, when the Shannons walked out the door, never to return. Maybe completing this ritual will give us the courage to start restoring this Big House.

We spend the day up at the Big House cleaning out the West Room, still full of paint tins, brushes, insulation, Liffey moving boxes. It's an exorcism of sorts, Geoffrey squooshing empty boxes so damp they collapse like deflated pastry dough, me stomping on bubble wrap, enjoying the *pop pop pop*. There remain a few boxes of stuff we had shipped over earlier in the year. But it's not laziness that keeps us from opening them, rather the fear of sadness from seeing the things that once meant so much to us at Magic Flute.

It is now the right time. We must look for the four brass candlesticks that lit our dinners in the Grove. Tonight we will place them in the windows and light them to welcome the spirits.

By three o'clock darkness is pulling in. And as I riffle around, just when I've convinced myself that the candlesticks are missing, I find them. They're inside a black garbage bag filled with Cherry Grove theater memorabilia. The flood of paper smells of the beach. Ferry schedules, copies of the *Fire Island News*, party invitations, programs of AIDS benefits, and posters of plays and musicals long gone. Shows I performed in. *Blithe Spirit*, *Candide*, *Damn Yankees*, *Six Red Dresses*, and *The Boyfriend*.

I start propping them up on the mantel. Soon the entire mantel is filled with the past. My past. Geoffrey's past. Our past on another island. Not so much our childhood bending before us, but our youth. When we walked out the door of Magic Flute, were we not as adventurous and sad as the Shannons walking out of this very room, leaving their Irish life behind to start a new life in England?

Sally Johnston loves to tell the story.

"O girl, it was the sorrow. With their little boys gone, they could bear it no longer. And it was the turkeys as well. All the turkeys they raised to sell in the market died. So they left. Left on the night boat with the clothes on their backs, leaving everything behind."

Tonight we will honor our dead and our old selves.

At six o'clock, we return to the Big House with beeswax candles and a little whiskey to warm our hearts and sprinkle on the hearth for the spirits. One by one we light the four candlesticks, one in each room: West Room, kitchen, box room, bedroom. The flames are unwavering in the dark, lighting this old house deep in the Irish countryside, a house we have put all our hopes, dreams, and money into.

That done, we drive down the laneway to the main road, first toward Bantry to see the lighted house *this way*, then toward Schull to see the house *that way*. *Faaaaaaaaaabuuuuuuulous!* we scream into the dark. And for a moment we're back on Fire Island. For a moment we're not over fifty. For a moment all is as it once was. For a moment we're possessed and screaming with delight with friends long gone. Screaming for the sheer joy of screaming.

Faaaaaaaaaabuuuuuulous! we scream and scream and scream into the dark all the way back up the laneway.

We stop the car by the cow gate and get out to take a long look. The house looks so beautiful. In the dark it doesn't look old. It doesn't look like a ruin. It looks like a wonderful old Irish house deep in the countryside. Behind the lighted windows, I see the spirits passing between rooms. Prancing up the stairs. Out to the scullery for the turf. Over to the fire to make the tea. The Shannons are ready to step into the future. They'll rise before dawn to take the boat train to Liverpool, the parents in travel clothes, Kathleen, their daughter, giddy with excitement.

Mammie is there, too. And Carey. For didn't the two of them, Alice Slattery and Denis Carey, sally forth from Ireland and sail to a new life in America? And did they not have me, Alice Marie Carey, born in New York City? And have I not returned to live in Ireland?

A Halloween rain is falling as Geoffrey and I enter the Big House. Drawn from the warmth of the fire at Faileth Not, Thomasina joins us. Geoffrey and I take a sup of whiskey. And for the millionth time we walk through this Big House that we still haven't a clue what to do with.

"Geoffrey," I say, "we're walking on the same bat shite we did three years ago."

The candles gleam as we go from West to box to bed to bed to barn to scullery, oohing and aahing. Oh yes, this is what the house must have looked like a hundred years ago. Look how the candlelight gleams on the stone. Look how it reflects on the glass. We'll figure out what to do with it. Someday we'll sleep here, cook here, make love here. Tonight is the beginning. Tonight we are waltzing with our dreams, and the unfulfilled dreams of the Shannons and Denis and Alice Carey.

Geoffrey and I stand in front of the fireplace of the West Room and raise our glasses in tribute to ourselves and our dead. I throw some whiskey on the hearth. Then we go back to Faileth Not to bank the fire and go to bed. When we wake up on All Saints' Day, we find our fire has not gone out.

The spirits were here as well.

The Lake isle of Innisfree

I will arise and go now, and go to Innisfree,
And a small cabin build there, of clay and wattles made: Nine
bean-rows will I have there, a hive for the honey-bee,
And live alone in the bee-loud glade.

And I shall have some peace there, for peace comes dropping slow,
Dropping from the veils of the morning to where the cricket sings;
There midnight's all a glimmer, and noon purple glow,
And evening full of the linnet's wings.

I will arise and go now, for always night and day
I hear lake water lapping with low sounds by the shore; While I
stand on the roadway, or on the pavements grey,
I hear it in the deep heart's core.

W. B. YEATS

Afterword
One for the Road

I HAVE A MEMORY ever emblazoned on my heart of my last night in the Magic Flute.

It's All Hallow's Eve. The house is packed up—except for a few candlesticks and the crystal hanging oil lamp, here since the 1930s, that we'll let the movers pack tomorrow morning.

I'm sitting up in bed, our lovely old bed in the summer bedroom, watching Geoffrey gently lower the lamp, extinguishing its flame for the last time in this house. The light is illuminating his face, transforming him into a figure in a Vermeer painting. And as I look at Geoffrey performing this most ancient of gestures, I wonder, could anything ever be as good as this again?

My life in Ireland is. But it's different than the vision people have of me sitting around reading books in front of a fire and sipping tea. Instead, I'm vacuuming spider webs that cover the old windows as the washing machine whirs away in the background. Granted, it's way down the way in a room romantically called the Boots Room. Somehow, the very concept of Ireland conveys a romance that precludes washing machines.

Except for the sound of bees buzzing around the room and hitting the windows trying to escape, and a light breeze rustling the trees, the drowsy washing machine is the only sound I hear on this early June day.

Everything is beautiful. A jug of pink jasmine-scented Louise Odier roses sits on the long table next to my laptop. Thomasina is reclining on Janie's chaise and giving herself a mid-morning bath. Even the Boots Room, with the row of green wellies, foul-weather gear, umbrellas, and winter wood stacked at the ready, is beautiful.

Geoffrey and I have accomplished what we set out to do in 1994: restore a ruined house and turn it into a simply beautiful one. Or should I say "houses"? The Big House, christened Summerhill, its original nineteenth-century name, is now completely restored. And the cottage, Faileth Not, is as beautiful as ever. Even so, the life I live here is not what I thought living in Ireland would be.

On that Thanksgiving Day in 1994, Geoffrey and I hadn't a clue what we were getting into—if we had, we could not have done what we did. We came to Ireland in search of Romance, found it, and bought a plantation full of it.

What we didn't buy was Reality—any whiff of reality dampens enthusiasm. But we soon learned that what charmed us (then and now) has consequences beyond sheer beauty, like grass grows and sheep eat just about everything.

Now you might say, "Oh come on, everyone knows grass grows."

And, of course, we knew that, but in our New York way.

That evening in 1994, as Geoffrey and I plodded around the fields, entranced by tall meadow grass dripping and glistening in the rain, we didn't *really* know that grass grows and grows and seeds everywhere.

Walking *New Yorker* covers that we are, it never entered our minds that Central Park's beautifully maintained Sheep's Meadow must be mowed regularly. Just as our three acres must be mowed and disposed of (whether we're in residence or not) so we can have our own Sheep's Meadow.

The joke is: In Ireland we have real sheep! There they are, blithely munching away (I can see them from the window) keeping the neighboring farmer's fields brusquely manicured.

There's an irony in paying someone to mow our grass when the sheep would do it for free, given half a chance and a hole in the fence. But they'd also snitch a few lagniappe treats, like, roses, lilacs, daffodils, and bay leaves. Yes, bay leaves.

Yet I must confess to a major handicap, a handicap insured to drop jaws on both sides of the Atlantic.

I can't drive.

I hitchhike.

And I love it.

When I'm here on my own I hitch every day. I've been doing it since 1997.

A few years ago, if asked to name things I'd never, ever do, I would have said getting tattooed, having my nose pierced, and hitchhiking. A city gal doesn't do that sort of thing.

Claudette Colbert, lifting her skirt and showing her gams on a country road may be one thing, but the vision of myself standing alone at the side of an Irish road is quite another. Mammie would die if she saw me. Miss D. never compromised her high standards of good taste to risk getting her shoes smudged in a beaten-up jalopy. Yet the fickle finger of fate was clearly aimed in my direction on the New Year of 1997.

Geoffrey and I had been away from Ireland since September and were dying to see Thomasina. So when we arrive on the winter solstice, we come bearing gifts. Cases of cat opium—Sheba and Fancy Feast—treats for this little cat I believe to be a gift from the fairies.

So thrilled are we to see Thomasina—no longer a kitten but a young cat—we feed her and feed her and feed her, an ill-advised thing to do, since her spaying operation is scheduled for the next day.

The vet should have told us (and we should have known) that any animal about to undergo anesthesia must do so on an empty stomach. And Thomasina's was full. The spaying was a cock-up. She hemorrhages, breaks stitches, and nearly dies.

Three times Thomasina escapes into the fields to die, as cats do when they know the jig is up. Three times we find her. And three times we drive over the mountains to Ballydehob where the vet sews her up again, again, and again.

On the third passage over the mountains, in the middle of the night, mind, it dawns on me that I can't drive. I have never even pictured myself behind the wheel of a car. Yet despite this handicap, and with Geoffrey returning to New York, I decide to stay alone in Ireland in this "the coldest winter in living memory" to nurse Thomasina back to health.

At five o'clock in the morning the day after Little Christmas, with the black Irish night still gripping the countryside and icicles dripping from the hawthorn trees, I stand at the cow gate waving Geoffrey down the lane-way realizing my life is about to take a turn. To get around I will have to learn to hitchhike.

It's easy enough, isn't it? Geoffrey and I see hitch-hikers all the time as we zoom down the road. There they stand, bedraggled lot that they are, with their thumbs out, knapsacks at side. And do we stop to share our upgraded rental car with scruffy kids who act mute, grunt, and smoke? No. We pass 'em by.

Yet here am I, about to do the same thing.

God knows I'm far from scruffy. Viewing my array of tweed jackets, I feel urged on by Stephen Dedalus, who said: "We simply must dress the character."

Me too. My first lesson in how to get picked up instantly is: Be spiffy.

But how will drivers know I'm going only a short way? How will they know I'm not some pain in the ass wanting a lift to Dublin? It's about a twenty-minute drive to Bantry, nothing really. But the windy eight miles is too long to walk since I'm not going on a hike. I'm just going to the bank and the butcher.

At two in the afternoon, the day Geoffrey left, with a weak winter sun losing to a rising ground frost, I start getting ready. The temperature is hovering around freezing, which in New York can be balmy, but in Ireland is miserable. With my favorite tweed jacket in hand, my egg yolk–yellow beret, and my *de rigueur* wellies (the pair I jazzed up with rhinestone clasps), I stop to consider what I am doing.

I feel more than a little foolish. And I'm damned nervous.

At this age of your life, Alice, you're doing what? Sophie du Plantier's murderer is still on the loose in West Cork. Wasn't she found murdered at the end of her laneway the night of the solstice? The murderer could be on the loose, looking for another woman—me.

I don't want to wind up assaulted, raped, or dead on the road. But bad things happen to women of all ages. I'm sturdy but small. If anything bad happens, I could get away if I could yank open the car door and jump out. Then again, I could brain myself doing this.

Christ almighty, Alice, banish these Hitchcockian fantasies or you'll never get up the nerve to get on the road. You should have taken Drivers Ed at Rhodes School like everyone else, but you didn't.

In a stroke of genius I realize what may help me is a sign simply saying "Bantry." That way the driver will know I'll be with him or her for a mere twenty minutes. I write BANTRY on a piece of cardboard. And with that I walk down the lane-way to the road, a twenty-minute walk in and of itself, on my maiden voyage where I will learn to depend on the kindness of strangers.

The R591 looms in front of me—a road I've never actually looked at from this perspective before. Hat on head, sign in hand, I wonder, *Where do I stand? The side our house is on or on the side with cars going to Bantry? If anything bad happens, at the get-go I mean, I'd best be standing on my side so I can run back up the lane-way. But the way these cars are going—Christ, they're fast—I better stand on the Bantry side.*

I cross the road and position myself by a telephone pole in a small curve where ongoing cars can see me way in advance and make the decision whether to do a girl a favor. There I stand, market basket between my legs, so the driver can see I'm just a local out on a few errands.

It's freezing. I'm freezing, yet old habits die hard. I reach into my breast pocket to daub on a slight smear of lip-gloss. Now, more than ever, it's important to look spiffy. I take my sign saying BANTRY, hold it straight out, and smile. I smile at the oncoming cars—my next lesson in the art of hitching.

There I stand freezing and smiling out on an empty road. The afternoon is drawing in and there are few cars. My concern has shifted from the fear of rape to the fear of not getting the newspapers. It's so late in the day they may be sold out. I make a note that if I continue to lead a life on the road, I must leave the house earlier.

As I contemplate the vagaries of time and tide waiting for no man, I see a car approach. Then I really smile. And the car slows down and stops.

As I run up a ways to get in, I see that my maiden voyage will take place in an old beat-up Ford with boxes and ropes and papers and plastic basins filling the back seat. There's so much stuff piled back there I can barely see the driver's arm pushing out the front door for me. But I note he's wearing a rumpled black suit jacket.

"Girleen" says he, "ye can climb in da're . . . sorry for d'mess. I'm a pig farmer see."

Now I ask you, how many people do you know who've been picked up by a pig farmer on their maiden voyage?

"It's fine, it's fine," I say, seating myself on a pile of old copies of the *Southern Star*. "You're very sweet to do this."

Big pause here.

". . . Bantry?"

"I can see that, girleen."

Not knowing what else to say I say, "My name is Alice and I live just up the way there."

"But ye'r not from 'round here. I can tell by ye'r accent."

"No, I'm from . . ."

Then I proceed to tell him my odyssey to Ireland—encapsulated into five minutes.

Another lesson learnt is drivers always want to know who you are and why you're here.

The old guy is silent. We've fifteen minutes to go. I don't think anything bad will happen to me except a hefty cleaning bill to rid my jacket of pig smell.

As we drive on, passing a barren stretch aptly called the "old bog road" I say, "What's your name?"

"Billy Cotter. I raise d'pigs now and I'm sorry about d'smell dare . . ."

"It's okay . . ."

"But I didn't always do dis. I was in d'Show Bands. Do ye remember d'Show Bands?"

"I do indeed."

In the '50s, '60s, even into the '70s—before the course of music changed forever with the Beatles—Irish Show Bands, their members dressed and coifed like Buddy Holly, toured the country thumping out Irish versions of country-western songs. When I was Alice M'rie, Mammie and I would occasionally have Father Bob drive us into Killarney on an evening to the Glen Eagle Hotel, where we'd sit in the lobby just to get a sound of them.

"What instrument did you play?"

"D'sax."

By now we've turned onto the main road with Bantry just five minutes away.

"It was a great time d'en. But it's all gone. Listen to Radio Kerry? Dey play d'bands now and den."

"Do you hear yourself?"

"Ee'ra, I keep listenin'."

Now we're circling Wolfe Tone Square. Billy Cotter lets me out. I make it in time for the papers. I never see him again.

That was seven years ago. Now I wouldn't change my life on the road for all the tea in China.

Friends have given up asking me if I'll ever learn to drive. But their pained expression still registers disappointment in my not pursuing this vehicular independence, as well as concern for my safety. Not that I didn't try. In 1998 I bought a teeny tiny old Renault from a man who picked me up on the road.

A fellow named Lofty, a New England history professor in Cork for the summer, was dying to get rid of his second-hand "Parisienne." We struck a deal. I gave him £400 and said I'd name the car after him. Then I waited for Geoffrey to arrive and smile, which he didn't. So shocked was he (and everyone else) that I'd buy such a heap of junk.

I could scarce get anyone into "Lofty" to teach me. No one could fit—Professor Lofty and I being on the small side. One who did try, a driving instructor I got from the phone book, ranted on and on about the glories of sobriety.

"Drink is the root of all evil, believe you me, my girl. Now you may think you know this old saying, but until you've experienced the hounds of hell snapping at your heels, you won't take the pledge."

On his lapel, the abstinence "pledge pin"—that of the Sacred Heart of Jesus, with a dagger piercing through it—gleams in the sun. And as we make our way round and round the Bantry parking lot where the lessons take place at eight in the morning—because it's empty—he tells me this over and over again.

"Mr. Mulrooney, I'm not a drinker. I don't even go to the pubs . . ."

"Nonetheless, girl. The devil is out there, right over there, in this very town."

He points to a hotel and its basement nightclub that is puzzlingly named Mozart.

"Kids come out of there puking their brains out every night."

I don't comment. Circling the parking lot, turning right when I'm positive I'm turning left, I realize I'm not cut out for a life at the wheel. Mammie's death on that side street in Astoria flashes brightly before me, yet I can't let it defeat me. To help myself, I write "left" and "right" on appropriate knuckles, just like Robert Mitchum has "love" and "hate" tattooed on his in *The Night of the Hunter*. But it's of little help.

Being at the helm of a car, the speed, the traffic, not knowing left from right, is scary. I could bring myself harm. Worse, I could hit, knock down, injure, or even kill someone by turning the wrong way. So when Mulrooney announces that he's off to a retreat in Mayo for prayer and contemplation, "Lofty" goes into retreat as well. We've let the grass grow tall around it.

Every year I make myself a new sign for Bantry. And every year I delight in meeting the Irish on the go. Sometimes those twenty minutes are my only social interaction in the day.

Being spiffy, smiley, and letting drivers know that I'm going just to Bantry ensures I have no trouble getting lifts. I'm picked up by rich and poor, sober and drunk, smelly and clean, men and women, old and young. Occasionally teens tell me I'm "cool."

Ireland is increasingly becoming a car culture with people running around like wild fire, but to where? Why? I stand on the road contemplating this. I stand on the road with my sign waiting for a stranger to be kind. I stand on the road with my sign waiting for a stranger to take a little piece of their time and share it with me.

I've come to think that people are grateful to have a stranger with them for twenty minutes of non-judgmental talk. Or maybe I should say love, for that's all I can give them:

The woman with swollen eyes, black and blue marks, a car full of screaming children who I promised I'd put in a word for with the BVM.

The lonely Dublin salesman on the road twenty days a month who said I had red hair like Ginger Rogers and who wanted to buy me a drink.

The old English woman and the old dog on her daily visit to her husband in the county "home." "It's hard, dearie, to be alone," she said.

The vet who reeked of vodka—bloody apparatus on the floor, dated surgical books on the dash board—speeding to a nearby farm to birth a mare.

All these people have shown kindness to a stranger.

Am I scared to still be doing this—at this age of my life? Sure, there's always an element of danger in entering into the unknown day after day. But I know I'm protected.

Long before I met Geoffrey, I had a summer fling with the Irish actor Patrick Magee, who was in New York trapped in a flop of a Broadway play and looking for comfort from someone from "home." Magee was from Donegal, so we hit it off. He'd recite Yeats to me. And I thought it oh so glamorous. At some point he told me that he had this thing, a blessing actually, called *baraka*.

Baraka was glamorous. It was Arabic. It mean't you were born with the luck of never being hurt or killed, even if you come very close to being so.

Magee liked it (as did I) because it was such a departure from our Roman Catholic backgrounds of sin and earning points towards redemption. You either have it or you don't. And I had it. That's what Magee said.

So I stand on the road with my sign and my *baraka*. I smile at the oncoming cars. No harm has come to me in these eight years. I feel blessed standing here, waiting for someone to be kind, knowing I can only repay this kindness by a smile, a word, a pat on the hand.

When I exit their cars I always say "Bless you."

Alice Carey
West Cork, Ireland
November 2004

acknowledgments

FRIENDS AND MENTORS who have already embarked on their "awfully big adventure" would pop into my head and pluck me up when a cup of tea wouldn't do the trick.

Specifically, Derek Jarman and Dennis Potter, who help me shape a vision of the world and lent me the words to describe it.

The wry eyes of Eric Schepard, David Baker, and my dear Brooks Peters, who would have been so proud of me.

My living muses, Bob Bent, Jack Dowling, and David La Greca, who read every word of every version and commented lavishly.

George Nicholson, whose steady hand never left the helm nor the phone.

Annetta Hanna, who certainly knew it when she saw it and had the style and the wisdom not to unduly muck around with it.

Charlotte Sheedy, who way back when told me I could write.

Maureen Barron, who helped shape an earlier version and taught me how to paragraph.

And my friends who simply asked how my work was coming along, and meant it—Tim Sweeney, Jed

Mattes, Father Brendan O'Rourke, Laura Dunlop, Ray Mann, Laurie Linton, Gilbert Parker, Michael J. Carroll, Liz Royles, Ronnie Payne, Sondra Ross, Francis Hines, Esther, and all the women at the pool.

And steadfastly ever there, Gordon Rogoff and Morton Lichter.

Of course, I not only acknowledge, but I am beholden to, Geoffrey Knox, my partner in life and in this adventure. Years ago, when Liliane Montevecchi won a Tony for the musical *Nine* and she thanked her husband for not interfering, I thought, That's it! But my Geoffrey has done far more that just not interfering. Geoffrey simply helped by always being there for me. That, and not interfering.

About the author

ALICE CAREY, a former substitute schoolteacher and musical-theater performer, has written for a variety of publications. She divides her time between New York City and West Cork, Ireland. She is at work on a second book, a memoir tentatively entitled "Marry of Burn."

Selected Seal Titles

The Beauvoir Sisters: An Intimate Look at How Simone and Hélène Influenced Each Other and the World by Claudine Monteil, translated from the French by Marjolijn de Jager. $14.95, 1-58005-110-3. Told by a close friend, this biography offers a startling glimpse into the artistic, personal, political, and intellectual lives of two very different sisters.

The F-Word: Feminism in Jeopardy by Kristin Rowe-Finkbeiner. $14.95, 1-58005-114-6. An astonishing look at the tenuous state of women's rights and issues in America, this pivotal book also incites women with voting power to change their situations.

No Hurry to Get Home: The Memoir of The New Yorker Writer Whose Unconventional Life and Adventures Spanned the Twentieth Century by Emily Hahn. $14.95, 1-58005-045-x. Hahn's memoir captures her free-spirited, charismatic personality and her inextinguishable passion for the unconventional life.

Pilgrimage to India: A Woman Revisits Her Homeland by Pramila Jayapal. $14.95, 1-58005-052-2. This eloquent and spirited book weaves together perceptive commentary on contemporary issues with her own profoundly moving journey of self-discovery.

The Pirate Queen: In Search of Grace O'Malley and Other Legendary Women of the Sea by Barbara Sjoholm. $15.95, 1-58005-109-x. A fascinating account of an intriguing Irish clan chieftan is joined by tales of cross-dressing sailors, medieval explorers, storm witches, and sea goddesses.

Private Matters: In Defense of the Personal Life by Janna Malamud Smith. $14.95, 1-58005-107-3. More pertinent than ever before, this modern history of privacy offers insights into the role of this increasingly fragile and elusive virtue.

Under Her Skin: How Girls Experience Race in America edited by Pooja Makhijani. $15.95, 1-58005-117-0. This diverse collection of personal narratives explores how race shapes, and sometimes shatters, live—as seen through the fragile lens of childhood.

Seal Press publishes many books of fiction and nonfiction by women writers. Please visit our website at www.sealpress.com.